TRADITIONS OF CHRISTIAN SPIRITUALITY

D0253459

PRAYER AND COMMUNITY

TRADITIONS OF CHRISTIAN SPIRITUALITY SERIES

At the Fountain of Elijah: The Carmelite Tradition
Wilfrid McGreal O. Carm.

Brides in the Desert: The Spirituality of the Beguines
Saskia Murk-Jansen

Eyes to See, Ears to Hear: An Introduction to Ignatian Spirituality
David Lonsdale

God's Lovers in an Age of Anxiety: The Medieval English Mystics
Joan M. Nuth

Journeys on the Edges: The Celtic Tradition
Thomas O'Loughlin

Mysticism and Prophecy: The Dominican Tradition
Richard Woods OP

The Poetic Imagination: An Anglican Spiritual Tradition
William Countryman

Poverty and Joy: The Franciscan Tradition
William J. Short OFM

Prayer and Community: The Benedictine Tradition
Columba Stewart OSB

The Spirit of Worship: The Liturgical Tradition
Susan J. White

Standing in God's Holy Fire: The Byzantine Tradition
John Anthony McGuckin

The Way of Simplicity: The Cistercian Tradition
Esther de Waal

PRAYER AND COMMUNITY

The Benedictine Tradition

COLUMBA STEWART OSB

SERIES EDITOR:
Philip Sheldrake

ORBIS BOOKS

Maryknoll, New York 10545

The Catholic Foreign Mission Society of America (Maryknoll) recruits and trains people for overseas missionary service. Through Orbis Books, Maryknoll aims to foster the international dialogue that is essential to mission. The books published, however, reflect the opinions of their authors and are not meant to represent the official position of the society.

First published in 1998 by
Darton, Longman and Todd Ltd.
1 Spencer Court
140–142 Wandsworth High Street
London SW18 4JJ
Great Britain

Published in the USA in 1998 by
Orbis Books
P.O. Box 308
Maryknoll, New York 10545–0308
U.S.A.

Fifth Printing, January 2004

Copyright © 1998 by Columba Stewart

ISBN 1–57075–219–2

All rights reserved. No part of this publication may be reproduced or transmitted in any form or by any means, electronic or mechanical, including photocopying, recording or any information storage or retrieval system, without prior permission in writing from the publishers.

Queries regarding rights and permissions should be addressed to the publishers.

Designed by Sandie Boccacci
Phototypeset in 10/13¼pt New Century Schoolbook
by Intype London Ltd
Printed and bound in Great Britain by
CPI Bath

Library of Congress Cataloging-in-Publication Data

Stewart, Columba.
    Prayer and community : the Benedictine tradition / Columba Stewart.
       p. cm.—(Traditions of Christian spirituality)
    Includes index.
    ISBN 1–57075–219–2 (paper)
    1. Benedict, Saint, Abbot of Monte Cassino. Regula.
    2. Benedictines—Spiritual life. I. Title. II. Series.
    BX3005.Z5S74   1998
    255′.1—dc21   98–21362
                                                    CIP

To my brothers of Saint John's Abbey.

In memory of
Father Michael Marx OSB (1913–1993)
Abbot Primate Jerome Theisen OSB (1930–1995).

CONTENTS

ABBREVIATIONS

CCM	*Corpus consuetudinum monasticarum*
RB	*Rule of Benedict*
RM	*Rule of the Master*

ACKNOWLEDGEMENTS

As always, my major debt is to my confrères at Saint John's Abbey who have taught me what I know about the monastic life. In addition, the following people read and commented on various drafts of this book: Joseph Feders OSB; Mary Forman OSB; Kathleen Norris; David Scotchie; Lorraine Mackay Stewart; Donald Tauscher OSB; Susan Wood SCL. I thank them for their clarity and their charity. I owe special thanks to Stephen and Gina Wolfe, who have taught me the meaning of hospitality.

PREFACE TO THE SERIES

Nowadays, in the western world, there is a widespread hunger for spirituality in all its forms. This is not confined to traditional religious people, let alone to regular churchgoers. The desire for resources to sustain the spiritual quest has led many people to seek wisdom in unfamiliar places. Some have turned to cultures other than their own. The fascination with Native American or Aboriginal Australian spiritualities is a case in point. Other people have been attracted by the religions of India and Tibet or the Jewish Kabbalah and Sufi mysticism. One problem is that, in comparison to other religions, Christianity is not always associated in people's minds with 'spirituality'. The exceptions are a few figures from the past who have achieved almost cult status such as Hildegard of Bingen or Meister Eckhart. This is a great pity, for Christianity East and West over two thousand years has given birth to an immense range of spiritual wisdom. Many traditions continue to be active today. Others that were forgotten are being rediscovered and reinterpreted.

It is a long time since an extended series of introductions to Christian spiritual traditions has been available in English. Given the present climate, it is an opportune moment for a new series which will help more people to be aware of the great spiritual riches available within the Christian tradition.

The overall purpose of the series is to make selected spiritual traditions available to a contemporary readership. The books seek to provide accurate and balanced historical and thematic treatments of their subjects. The authors are also conscious of the need to make connections with contemporary experience and values without being artificial or reducing a tradition to one dimension. The authors are well-versed in reliable scholarship about the traditions they describe. However, their intention is that the books should be fresh in style and accessible to the general reader.

One problem that such a series inevitably faces is the word 'spirituality'. For example, it is increasingly used beyond religious circles and does not necessarily imply a faith tradition. Again, it could mean substantially different things for a Christian and a Buddhist. Within Christianity itself, the word in its modern sense is relatively recent. The reality that it stands for differs subtly in the different contexts of time and place. Historically, 'spirituality' covers a breadth of human experience and a wide range of values and practices.

No single definition of 'spirituality' has been imposed on the authors in this series. Yet, despite the breadth of the series there is a sense of a common core in the writers themselves and in the traditions they describe. All Christian spiritual traditions have their source in three things. First, while drawing on ordinary experience and even religious insights from elsewhere, Christian spiritualities are rooted in the Scriptures and particularly in the Gospels. Second, spiritual traditions are not derived from abstract theory but from attempts to live out gospel values in a positive yet critical way within specific historical and cultural contexts. Third, the experiences and insights of individuals and groups are not isolated but are related to the wider Christian tradition of beliefs, practices and community life. From a Christian perspective, spirituality is not just concerned with prayer or even with narrowly religious activities. It concerns the whole of human life, viewed in terms of a conscious relationship with God, in Jesus Christ, through the indwelling of the Holy Spirit and within a community of believers.

The series as a whole includes traditions that probably would not have appeared twenty years ago. The authors themselves have been encouraged to challenge, where appropriate, inaccurate assumptions about their particular tradition. While conscious of their own biases, authors have nonetheless sought to correct the imbalances of the past. Previous understandings of what is mainstream or 'orthodox' sometimes need to be questioned. People or practices that became marginal demand to be re-examined. Studies of spirituality in the past frequently underestimated or ignored the role of women. Sometimes the treatments of spiritual traditions were culturally one-sided because they were written from an uncritical western European or North Atlantic perspective.

However, any series is necessarily selective. It cannot hope to do full justice to the extraordinary variety of Christian spiritual traditions. The principles of selection are inevitably open to question. I hope that an appropriate balance has been maintained between a sense of the likely readership on the one hand and the dangers of narrowness on the other. In the end, choices had to be made and the result is inevitably weighted in favour of traditions that have achieved 'classic' status or which seem to capture the contemporary imagination. Within these limits, I trust that the series will offer a reasonably balanced account of what the Christian spiritual tradition has to offer.

As editor of the series I would like to thank all the authors who agreed to contribute and for the stimulating conversations and correspondence that sometimes resulted. I am especially grateful for the high quality of their work which made my task so much easier. Editing such a series is a complex undertaking. I have worked closely throughout with Morag Reeve of Darton, Longman & Todd and Robert Ellsberg of Orbis Books. I am immensely grateful to them for their friendly support and judicious advice. Without them this series would never have come together.

PHILIP SHELDRAKE
Sarum College, Salisbury

INTRODUCTION

This book is about the spirituality of the Benedictine monastic tradition. Inevitably, the sixth-century *Rule of Benedict* is central to this study. The *Rule* means little, however, unless it is lived. Fifteen hundred years of Benedictine life have created a breathtaking variety of interpretations of the *Rule* and patterns of living it. Because of this, I write about both Benedict's teaching in his *Rule* and its subsequent development by his spiritual heirs. The emphasis on application and interpretation makes sense, for Benedictine spirituality is pre-eminently practical.

I have kept in mind three groups of prospective readers: my Benedictine brothers and sisters; those who already know something about the Benedictine tradition, such as oblates, retreatants and friends; those who have little direct acquaintance with either the *Rule* or its lived expression but who want to know what Benedictine life contributes to Christian spirituality. I have tried to include something for all of you in this book and hope that I have excluded none.

I write as a male and North American Benedictine living in a large community with a history of pastoral and educational work. My horizons are continually expanded by working closely with the Benedictine women of our sister monastery and by regularly visiting communities of men and women both in the United States and abroad. I have tried to be inclusive in my overview of Benedictine life but freely admit the limitations of my own perspective. Because Benedictine spirituality is so rooted in practice, and practices vary from monastery to monastery, generalizing is dangerous. One runs the risk of being too inclusive for some tastes and too narrow for others. I have tried to strike a balance, and ask forgiveness when I am seen to have failed.

The plan of the book is straightforward, beginning in Chapter 1 with historical context, the *Rule of Benedict* and Benedict himself. Chapters 2-6 take up the major elements of Benedictine life and spirituality: prayer, obedience and humility, the structures of common life, monastic asceticisms, stages of life. Running throughout the book is the theme of life in community. The genius of Benedict was to situate the individual search for God within a communal context that shaped as well as supported the quest. For him community was not simply the place where one seeks God but its vital means. This is perhaps his most important message for modern Christians, especially those in western countries where autonomy has become the ideal pattern for life. In the conclusion I write briefly of Benedictine spirituality as a word offered to all seekers on the Christian way. The list of recommended reading will provide further information about the texts I refer to or quote, and will suggest possibilities for further pursuit. I have not included references to critical editions of primary sources except where no translations exist. Such information can be found in the translations or in the usual reference guides.

Because I refer constantly to the *Rule of Benedict*, readers of this book may find it helpful to obtain a copy of the *Rule* for reference. It is not absolutely essential to read the *Rule* and this study side-by-side but doing so will increase comprehension for those who do not already know the *Rule* well. Several editions and translations are available and any will do; the translations here are my own, informed by the several versions commonly available. I used the Latin text of J. Neufville found most conveniently in Timothy Fry, *et al.*, *RB 1980*.

Writing this book has been challenging but joyful, as

monastic life itself should be. With God's help and the teaching of Saint Benedict, may we be brought together to everlasting life (*RB* 72.12).

COLUMBA STEWART OSB
Saint John's Abbey
Feast of the Triumph
of the Cross, 1997

1. UNDERSTANDING BENEDICT

MONASTICISM BEFORE BENEDICT

When Benedict became a monk around the year 500, the monastic life was already well-established.[1] Christian asceticism was as old as the Church, practised by women and men who felt called to lives of prayer and spiritual discipline. The New Testament speaks already of an order of widows devoted especially to prayer. Informal ascetical communities, often home-based, had long been part of the Christian landscape in places as far apart as Rome, Asia Minor and Syria. Among Syriac-speaking Christians in upper Mesopotamia, for example, asceticism had a venerable place at the very heart of the Church in the 'Daughters and Sons of the Covenant', who lived celibately among their fellow Christians. In the Latin west there was a tradition of female ascetical life among wealthy Roman women like Marcella and their households.

What we typically call 'monasticism', an organized asceticism practised by individuals or groups, became prominent during the fourth century. A series of compelling figures, aided by pious publicists, caught the Christian imagination in both east and west and inspired thousands to follow them. The most famous of all was Antony the Great of Egypt, who had a brilliant biographer in Athanasius, Bishop of Alexandria. Antony and the hermit ('anchoritic') life he typified became one of the classic models of monasticism. The tradition established by him can be met most vividly in the pithy sayings of the Egyptian and Palestinian *abbas* and *ammas*. Their titles, of Aramaic origin, mean 'father' and 'mother', highlighting the spiritual parenting done by these extraordinary men and women.[2]

In the fourth century more institutional forms of communal asceticism emerged of the kind traditionally called 'monastic'.[3] In Egypt, communal asceticism was associated particularly with Pachomius, a southern Egyptian monk who began as a hermit. He developed a model for common life inspired by the early Christian community of Jerusalem as described in the Acts of the Apostles. In central Asia Minor, Basil the Great – who was taught the ascetical way of life by his mother and sister, who had turned the family home into a religious community – worked closely with established communities of men and women. His so-called *Long* and *Short Rules* summarized the theological and practical guidance he provided.

Throughout Italy and Gaul (modern France) various forms of ascetical life blossomed in the fourth century. Paulinus and his wife Therasia took vows of celibacy and lived the monastic life at Nola in Italy; the former soldier, Martin of Tours, established a community in western Gaul. In North Africa, Augustine of Hippo founded communities of men and women and wrote a basic rule of life for them. But these were only the famous ones: there were many, many more. In southern Gaul monasticism looked to Egypt for inspiration, and the island monastery of Lérins generated a series of monastic rules which would have a strong influence on Benedict. John Cassian, a great monastic traveller and theologian, settled in Marseilles early in the fifth century and wrote a series of *Institutes* and *Conferences* adapting earlier traditions to the conditions of monasticism in Gaul.[4]

In the fourth and fifth centuries the trend in Christian ascetical life was toward greater structure and regulation. Often the pressure came from outside, as bishops sought to formalize the place of asceticism in the life of the Church. Their motives were partly regulatory, to ensure that these men and women were under episcopal supervision. But ascetical communities had also reached a stage of theological and institutional development where clear ties to the larger Christian community had become more and more important. There were losses from the growing institutionalization of asceticism, particularly for women who became more regulated by an ecclesiastical hierarchy in which they had no formal place. Even for male monasteries, however, relations with bishops have rarely been uninteresting.

Latin monasticism was partial to the idea of a 'rule' upon which a community could base its life. The lived experience of a common rule will concern us in a later chapter. Here we can note that by the early sixth century there were several rules being used in western monasteries. These were supplemented by biographies of famous monastic founders or teachers and compendia such as Cassian's works. Latin monasteries had access to Pachomian, Basilian and other eastern materials in translation and these helped to shape self-understanding and the texts expressive of it. There was no conviction that a single rule had to be used forever or by everyone. Rules were rewritten, freely circulated and adapted.

THE RULE OF BENEDICT

In the early sixth century an Italian monk about whom we know nothing besides the epithet 'the Master' wrote a lengthy and frequently idiosyncratic rule that drew heavily from the earlier traditions. This odd but interesting document would have remained a monastic curiosity had it not become the principal source for the text we know as the *Rule of Benedict*.[5] Despite his debt to the Master, Benedict shows himself to be both a skilful editor and original thinker. His rule is only about a third as long as the *Rule of the Master* but he was able to retain its spiritual core while rigorously excluding the excursuses which amuse and exasperate the modern reader. The influence of Cassian, especially in the sections tributary to the Master, is manifest. In those chapters proper to Benedict, Augustine's emphasis on charity shines through. Both the Master and Benedict knew the Christian and monastic literature commonly available in their day. Their reading strongly influenced their writing. Benedict's *Rule* contains almost forty identifiable (though unattributed) quotations from other texts and dozens more possible allusions.[6] Though an original work, it is also deeply traditional. What Benedict provides is an interpretation and application of previous monastic experience.

Most striking to the modern reader of the *Rule* are the hundreds of quotations from, and allusions to, the Bible. Recent editions of the *Rule* print the biblical material in italic type, which is helpful for identification but misleading in suggesting that Benedict uses biblical passages simply as proof-texts or supporting material. In some places, especially the early chapters of the *Rule*, the biblical quotations carry the narrative line. Benedict develops his argument through juxtaposition of biblical texts, and to skim over them as if they were references rather than integral to the argument is to miss much of his teaching as well as his way of integrating the fruits of his *lectio divina*, 'sacred reading', into his spiritual teaching.

The *Rule of Benedict* consists of four major sections. The first is foundational. Its lengthy Prologue, borrowed from the Master but with new opening lines adapted by Benedict from another source, invites the individual Christian to follow the Lord's call to monastic life. The first seven chapters present the cenobitic framework of rule and abbot/superior (*RB* 1–3), followed by a primer of monastic spirituality consisting of chapters on the 'Tools of Good Works' (*RB* 4), obedience (*RB* 5), conservation of speech (*RB* 6) and humility (*RB* 7). This section is based largely on the first ten chapters of the *Rule of the Master*.

The second major section, chapters 8–20, describes the structure and content of liturgical prayer, concluding with a few brief points about the theology and practice of prayer (*RB* 19–20). The third section outlines the structures and practices of the common life (*RB* 20–67). The Master's influence is still detectable, but much less marked than in the first seven chapters. The final section, consisting of the last six chapters, has no parallel in the *Rule of the Master*. There Benedict revisits the basic theology of monastic life with a particular emphasis on love. These chapters are especially cherished by Benedictines for the more direct access they provide to Benedict's own experience of the monastic life.

Benedict's *Rule* proved popular for both men and women. However, they felt the same freedom Benedict had to adapt and borrow from other rules, and his rule became a source rather than a norm. It was often used in combination with others, especially the harsher *Rule of Columban* with its Celtic roots. Only in the ninth century as part of the reform work of the Carolingian empire did the *Rule of Benedict* begin to acquire the exclusive and normative status it would come to have in the monastic west. The significance of this development for western cultural and religious history has been incalculable.

In the rest of this book we will work with Benedict's teaching in the *Rule*, its later interpretation and modern application. In Chapter 4 we will explore further the use and adaptation of the *Rule* by monastic men and women. Now we need to learn what we can about Benedict himself.

BENEDICT

Like most early monks, Benedict resists our desire to know about him. The *Rule* itself tells us nothing about its author, not even a name. Every known manuscript of the *Rule*, however, attributes it to 'Benedict'. Devotion to the life and deeds of this elusive figure has been almost entirely shaped by the stories recounted in the second book of Gregory the Great's *Dialogues*, written about fifty years after Benedict's death. Gregory devotes an entire book to Benedict, whom he calls *vir Dei*, 'the Man of God'. Gregory notes Benedict's authorship of a rule for monks outstanding for its discretion – by which we should understand insight and moderation – and for its 'luminous' language (*Dial.* 2.36). Gregory directs his readers to that rule (generally accepted to be the same *Rule of Benedict* we know) but does not quote from it in the *Dialogues*. In this rule, Gregory assures us, we will learn more about Benedict's character and life, for the holy man could not have lived otherwise than he taught. Benedict himself reminds the abbot/ superior to work hard at such integrity of life and teaching, lest a fatal credibility gap open between words and deeds (*RB* 2.11–15).

We are still left wondering how Benedict gained the experience and insight manifest in his *Rule*. Gregory helps with a series of vignettes of Benedict's early life. Scholarly consensus is that while Gregory surely embellishes the facts, he was doubtless working from information provided by those who had actually known Benedict. Gregory names four of his sources, two of them successors of Benedict as abbot of Monte Cassino, a third the abbot of Subiaco, and the fourth a disciple of Benedict who became abbot of a monastery in Rome. Such precision encourages our trust in the basic outline of the story even if not in its details.

Gregory tells us that Benedict had 'an old man's heart' even from his youth. As Gregory tells it, however, Benedict's passage from youth to mature adulthood was as difficult as it is for many people. Born around 480 or 490 into a free family in the region of Nursia (now Norcia), north-east of Rome, Benedict was sent to study in Rome. This lad from the provinces was scandalized by the worldliness of life in the capital. Rather than immerse himself in the opportunities before him (as the young Augustine had done in Carthage), Benedict reacted by renouncing his studies, family and inheritance 'to please God alone' in the monastic life. Gregory observes that Benedict withdrew from secular life 'knowingly ignorant and wisely uninstructed' (*Dial.* 2, Prol.). Benedict was certainly no philosopher or pedant. His education henceforth would be entirely biblical and theological, informed by his prayer and grounded in monastic experience.

Benedict's initial break from home and society was not total. Although he sought the 'desert', i.e., an isolated place for spiritual retirement, he took his governess with him. They settled east of Rome at a church in Effide, the modern town of Affile. There Benedict performed the first of the miracles attributed to him by Gregory. His nanny had broken a borrowed sieve or threshing-tray (the unusual Latin word is ambiguous), which Benedict repaired through prayer and tears.[7] The fame which followed this impressive act pushed Benedict to his final break from the past. Leaving behind both nanny and town, he found solitude nearby at Sublacus (modern Subiaco; the name refers to artificial lakes created by Nero, now destroyed). In this region of steep wooded hills and cold streams, Benedict found a small cave in which to lead the anchoritic life.

Most modern pilgrims find the small monastery later built above this cave to speak more of Benedict's time and experience than does the massive abbey at his later home of Monte Cassino. The cave contains a link to another age of religious life in the portrait of St Francis of Assisi painted on its wall. This is the earliest known portrait of the one who broke definitively from the monastic pattern identified so completely in his day with Benedict's *Rule*.

Supplied with a monastic habit, food and occasional company by a monk named Romanus, Benedict practised the hermit's life so assiduously that he even lost track of liturgical time. He had to be reminded of Easter by a visiting priest who turned up with a festal meal. That cave at Sublacus was Benedict's monastic crucible, in which he faced the usual temptations of flesh and spirit. Gregory notes that desires of the flesh require strict vigilance until the fires die back with age. After fifty, he claims, the fever passes; with the grace of age one can become a 'teacher (*doctor*) of the soul' (*Dial.* 2.2). Such, of course, would Benedict become: but not yet.

Benedict's path from solitude to community life was arduous. Others recognized his holiness, and monks of a nearby monastery prevailed upon him to become their spiritual father. Still young and inexperienced, he played the role of zealot and enforcer in a community unprepared for change. It was a disaster. Gregory comments, 'they found it hard to let go what they had thought about with their old minds in order to ponder new things.' Blaming one another for having nominated this fanatic to be their abbot, they finally agreed on one thing: to poison him.

As it turned out, Benedict's prayer was able to break vessels as well as mend them. When the rebels proffered him the poisoned carafe, he made the sign of the cross in blessing and it shattered. Rising to take leave of the conspirators, he remarked upon the incompatibility between them, advising them to 'go and look for a father according to your own tastes, because after this you cannot count on me' (*Dial.* 2.3). It is a remarkable understatement and a fine exit line. We find a curious echo of this experience – or perhaps Gregory found inspiration for it – in Benedict's warning lest a community choose to elect a superior in accord with its vices (*RB* 64.3). In this passage from the *Dialogues* Benedict seems positively to advise it, having almost paid a very high price for that community's failed aspirations of virtue.

Gregory seems somewhat embarrassed by Benedict's flight from that community. He defends it by arguing that the saint's soul was endangered by such an impossible situation. Frustration, distraction and discouragement were therefore inevitable unless he escaped. Benedict himself notes that the superior must not be 'restless or troubled, not extreme or stubborn, not jealous or oversuspicious, for then there will be no peace' (*RB* 64.16). So it was for him the first time around. Gregory also notes that Benedict's talents were wasted on such a hopeless situation.

The reality was surely more painful and formative than Gregory allows. Benedict was not the first cenobitic leader to have a disastrous first run. Pachomius, the Egyptian monk considered the originator of the cenobitic life, comes immediately to mind as another monastic founder who learned from catastrophe. After months of misery, he finally chased the first members of his monastery out the gate while brandishing an iron bolt to show them he meant business.[8] It is difficult not to attribute Benedict's compassionate remarks about the monastic superior in Chapter 64 of the *Rule* to the seasoning and wisdom of his own experience.

Benedict's return to solitude was short-lived, for Gregory tells us that he established around himself in the valley of Sublacus twelve monasteries of twelve monks each. Each monastery had a spiritual father, but some monks Benedict kept near himself for special instruction. Among the young men of noble Roman families entrusted to his care were Maur and Placid, the most famous of Benedict's disciples. Gregory relates stories from this period laden with biblical typology to establish Benedict's claim to the succession of prophets and apostles (*Dial.* 2.8).

Benedict's struggle against sin and temptation continued. As the *Life of Antony* reminds us, the vividness of the Enemy's attacks increases as one grows in virtue. Gregory claims that Benedict reached the stage of direct combat with the 'master of evil' (cf. *RB* 1.5) and needed a change of venue for the struggle. Troubles with an envious neighbouring priest contributed to Benedict's desire to move on, which he did probably around 530. He chose the mountain top of Casinum, familiar to us as Monte Cassino, where a temple of Apollo stood in a sacred grove. Benedict razed both temple and grove, built two oratories on the site, and began to preach to the local populace. It was the beginning of Benedictine pastoral outreach. The devil, Gregory tells us, could not bear such an incursion on his territory, and was reduced to plaintive appeals: 'Oh cursed one [*maledicte*], not blessed one [*benedicte*]: what business have you with me, why do you persecute me?' (*Dial.* 2.8). The question, familiar from the Gospels, had also been addressed to Antony the Great by the devil, who had come to complain about the crowds of monks invading his territory in the desert (*Life of Antony*, ch. 41).

The community Benedict established exists to this day, though the site was abandoned for some 125 years shortly after his death. The great abbey on the hilltop, rebuilt after its destruction in World War II, gives us little idea of the modest complex Benedict would have built using materials from the razed temple. Most of the stories Gregory relates of Benedict are set at Monte Cassino, and it was there that he wrote his *Rule*. Gregory records and interprets far too many of Benedict's deeds for us to ponder here. Only three can detain us: Benedict's contest of mind and heart with his sister Scholastica, his mystical vision of the whole world caught up in a single ray of light, and his death.

The story of Scholastica and Benedict is perhaps the most famous in the *Dialogues*. Meeting for their annual visit, the two siblings spent the day in praise of God and in holy conversation. As night came on, Benedict prepared to leave. Scholastica asked him to stay the night and discuss the joys of heaven. Benedict's stern devotion to rules (a throwback to his first abbacy?) leads to a shocked protest at her impertinence. Her reply is prayer rather than argument. She bows her head, prays with copious tears, and the skies imitate her example by pouring forth torrential rain. Her brother is shocked all the more by this brazen defiance of his authority and the appeal to a higher one: 'May almighty God forgive you, sister! What have you done?' She responds with the astringent *gravitas* Benedict had used with the monks who tried to poison him: 'I asked you, and you did not want to listen to me; I asked my Lord, and he answered me. Now go then, if you can: leave me and return to your monastery' (*Dial.* 2.33). Of course, he could not. The point of the story is not so much the power of prayer with tears (though Benedict liked the combination), but the power of love: Scholastica's was the greater. Benedict, like the eastern monk and writer Gregory of Nyssa,[9] had to defer to the deeper wisdom of his sister.

Scholastica was not Benedict's only partner in spiritual dialogue. Servandus, abbot of a monastery in Campania, would visit regularly to share 'sweet words of life' about the 'heavenly homeland' (cf. *RB* 73.8). During one of these visits, as Servandus lay sleeping in the room below, Benedict rose in the night to pray at the window of his tower room. He saw a bright light come down from heaven and illumine the night, shining 'amidst the darkness'. As he gazed into the splendour he found the entire world brought before his eyes 'as if gathered into a single ray' of light, and saw the soul of a bishop he knew being carried to heaven in a sphere of fire. Such mystical ravishment alarmed him, and he called Servandus' name several times. Frantic at this unexpected call, Servandus came up immediately but could see only a small part of the light. Even that was enough to stupefy him (*Dial.* 2.35).

Gregory interprets the experience as a glimpse of the 'light of the Creator', that divine luminescence prized by later Byzantine mystics as the pinnacle of contemplative possibility. Caught up into such a vision, Benedict was simultaneously taken 'above himself' and into an inner vastness where the things of this world, formerly so impressive, now seemed insignificant. This singular experience of seeing as God sees marks the greatness of soul given by grace to the 'Man of God'. Benedict evokes such enlargement of spirit in his Prologue: a monastic lifetime of running on the path of the commandments will so exercise the heart that it will 'expand with the inexpressible delight of love' (*RB* Prol. 49).

Benedict's own life was shaped by that divine light he prized so much (cf. *RB* Prol. 9,13,43). It is fitting, then, that his death was marked by a vision granted to his disciples of a pathway rising to heaven strewn with carpets and 'shining with innumerable lights' (*Dial.* 2.37). The death itself, Gregory tells us, occurred in the oratory of the monastery. After receiving communion, he died standing with his arms lifted in prayer by the hands of his brothers.

He who had begun as a solitary and zealot had become a thoroughly social monk. The most vivid stories of his life involve his spiritual interlocutors, Scholastica and Servandus. Even at the heights of mystical experience he took note of a friend's soul on its way to heaven. He died relying on his brothers' strength for the prayer he could no longer offer alone. Whatever Gregory's own purpose in presenting such a Benedict, the account rings true to what we find in the *Rule*. It is to the *Rule*, then, that we now turn. Two fundamental insights govern all that Benedict writes of the monastic life, and we begin with those: the divine presence is everywhere, and Christ is to be met in other people.

MINDFULNESS OF THE PRESENCE OF GOD

Awareness of the presence of God pervades the *Rule*.[10] No cosy intimacy between equals, this is very much a relationship of awe and utter dependence. Humility, the central monastic virtue, begins in 'fear of the Lord', which simply means acknowledging the divine omnipresence and acting accordingly. The corresponding vice is forgetting that one stands before God. One must 'flee forgetfulness and always be mindful of what God has commanded' (*RB* 7.10–11). Thus Benedict's emphasis on listening and on *lectio divina*: these are ways of mindfulness, of attuning the spiritual senses to the divine presence.

At times the stress falls on God's mindfulness of us, for Benedict tells us that God is watching us always and everywhere.[11] But equally, he emphasizes the obligation to make oneself known to God, the superior and spiritual elders.[12] The ideal is mutual awareness, not penal supervision. The imperative of openness, of transparency before God and others, links Benedict to a central theme of the early monastic tradition (see Chapter 5). Such openness rests entirely upon faith. Terror or constraint cannot compel it, and only trust nurtured and sustained by grace can bring it forth.

SEEING CHRIST IN OTHERS

Benedict's teaching on awareness of God finds a focal point in his Christology. At the core of monastic life must be encounter with Jesus Christ. Christ pervades the *Rule* from Prologue to final chapter. Benedict's faith in Christ is no surprise, but it does have distinctive outlines. His Christology was 'high'. He speaks comfortably of Christ as God, and indeed never uses the name 'Jesus'. He had a robustly orthodox sixth-century understanding of a divine saviour.

Benedict secures the centrality of Christ with phrases such as 'prefer nothing to the love of Christ', 'hold nothing more precious than Christ'.[13] Every aspect of life is to be governed by the principle of acting 'in the love of Christ'.[14] The Latin is ambiguous, tolerant of both the passive and active meanings of 'love from Christ' or 'love for Christ'. There is little real difference. All that we do for Christ we have already received from him.

Benedict's utter faith in the divine Son of God casts into even sharper relief his insight that this divine Christ is to be found and even adored in other human beings. His incarnate presence was not limited to Jesus of Nazareth, but remains among us in the monastic superior, the sick, the guest, the poor: a list so inclusive as to signify Christ's presence in all whom one meets. This is why in many monasteries the members process into the church in pairs, bow together to the altar, and then bow to one another in veneration of Christ.

Although the monastic superior is reckoned as 'holding the place of Christ' (*RB* 2.2, 63.13) as teacher and shepherd, Benedict's other examples of finding Christ in one's neighbours have to do with service and hospitality. The sick are served as Christ, according to Christ's own command (Matt. 25:35–40). Similarly, guests are welcomed as Christ. Benedict takes things deeper, however, urging a transparency before the other in recognition of the Christ who is met. Humility is to be shown to guests in a bow or prostration, which for Benedict were not merely formal gestures. The icon of humble self-awareness he paints in his chapter on humility, which is the very heart of his spiritual theology, depicts someone standing with head bowed in total acknowledgement of sinfulness, as if already before Christ in judgement (*RB* 7.62–6). That picture of someone who no longer has anything to hide from the Lord should guide our reading of Benedict's instructions about hospitality.

In receiving the guest as Christ, a Benedictine is standing before Christ with humble transparency. The Christ met in others is the same Christ who sustains all of one's life. The first response, then, is not 'can I help you?', but adoration of the Christ who has just arrived. Thus Benedict has the superior and community sing this verse after washing the feet of the guests: 'We have received, O God, your mercy in the midst of your temple' (Ps. 48:9). On the basis of this recognition, the practical needs of food, rest, and lodging can then be addressed. Benedict links the 'humility' (*humilitas*) of the one receiving the guest (*RB* 53.6) to the 'kindness' (*humanitas*) manifested in material hospitality (*RB* 53.9). The mindfulness of humility underlies the practice of service.

The rest of this book explores how these basic themes play out in monastic practice, beginning with the ways of mindfulness in prayer.

2. WAYS OF PRAYER AND MINDFULNESS

BENEDICTINE PRAYER

Benedict presents a simple theology of prayer: 'We believe that the divine presence is everywhere ... We should believe this all the more, without any doubt whatsoever, when we attend to the divine work' (*RB* 19.1–2). The 'divine work' is the liturgy of the hours, and by extension, all prayer. The monastic attitude toward prayer is not supposed to be *different* from that toward the rest of life, but *more so*. We are, Benedict says, to come before the 'Lord God of the universe' with *all* humility and *total* devotion (*RB* 20.2). As we shall see in Chapter 3, 'humility' is Benedict's way of characterizing mature self-awareness.

Prayer is the most fundamental of the spiritual practices that cultivate mindfulness of the divine presence, and the many forms of monastic prayer, communal and private, all centre on the biblical Word. The Bible was the source and context of early monastic prayer. Ancient nuns and monks were awash in biblical words and images. They read the Bible assiduously, had it read to them daily, memorized huge chunks of it, sang it at the canonical hours of prayer, repeated it with heart and mouth while working or travelling. Smaragdus, the first major commentator on the *Rule of Benedict*, quoted another monastic rule as saying, 'while on the outside the hands are occupied with work, on the inside the heart becomes sweet through meditating the psalms with the tongue and remembering the scriptures.'[1]

Everywhere we look for hints of Benedict's spirituality, we

find the Bible: in common and personal prayer, in spiritual reading and study, in the words he used to describe the fundamental monastic virtues of obedience and humility. The Word, for Benedict, meant pre-eminently Christ, the divine Word speaking through the Bible and met in other people. Learning to recognize the presence of Christ means discovering that the monastic path is the same as his, a self-emptying that makes room for God and for others.

Therefore, the prayerful encounter with the Bible called *lectio divina*, 'sacred reading', is the hallmark of Benedictine spirituality. The liturgical prayer for which Benedictine monasticism is best known is the ecclesial and communal side of each individual's *lectio divina*. Common prayer is nurtured and deepened by private prayer, just as private prayer is energized by corporate experience of the Word in the liturgy. To see *lectio* as fundamental to all Benedictine prayer does not downplay the communal liturgy but points to its heart, the unifying Word.

THE WORK OF GOD

The backbone of Benedictine prayer is the daily series of communal liturgical gatherings Benedict calls the 'Work of God'. In the *Rule* he lays out a detailed pattern of eight such 'offices' per day. He expected his monks to rise early, while it was still night, for a comparatively long service of psalms and readings called Vigils. They did not go back to bed afterwards; the ascetical practice of 'broken sleep', i.e., rising in the middle of the night for prayer and returning to bed afterwards, was not part of Benedict's plan. In the long nights of winter there was time after the vigil office for study and prayer; in the summer the dawn office of Lauds followed almost immediately. Benedict provided for four brief offices scattered throughout the day (Prime, Terce, Sext, None), an evening office (Vespers) and a brief bedtime office (Compline). It would seem that his monks spent between three-and-a-half and four hours per day in common prayer.

Each office consisted mostly of psalms, with brief readings (longer ones at Vigils), hymns and prayers added on. Sunday and feast-day offices were longer, including a supplemental group of biblical canticles and a Gospel reading at Vigils. Despite his intricate instructions (eleven chapters) he allows that someone might come up with a better schema, though he insists that the norm must always be a complete cycle through the Psalter each week (*RB* 18).

Benedict's monks still practised the ancient custom of following each psalm of the Liturgy of the Hours with an interval for silent prayer. Such prayer requires attention and focus. Benedict writes that private prayer should be 'brief and pure' unless prolonged by grace, and adds that the communal prayerful response to the Word should always be brief (*RB* 20.4–5). Benedict knew Cassian's vivid description of what happens when the silent intervals are prolonged to the point that attentiveness becomes distraction and, finally, drowsy stupor.[2]

Benedict gives us his understanding of the Work of God in two key phrases. One of them echoes his bottom-line saying about Christ: 'prefer nothing to the Work of God' (*RB* 43.3). This dictum comes as a warning against tardiness, but its echo of 'prefer nothing to the love of Christ' (*RB* 4.21; cf. 72.11) would not have been missed. The Work of God is the time and place of mindfulness of God par excellence; to miss it is to miss a precious opportunity of encounter with the One who is sought through the monastic way of life. At the Work of God, Benedict notes, we stand in the sight of God and the angels. This is always so, of course, but is especially true at the Work of God, when there must be a special effort that 'our minds are in harmony with our voices' (*RB* 19.7). The theological implications of standing already in the heavenly choir would have impressed Benedict's early readers, who had a livelier sense than we do that Christian life is preparation for Heaven.

Until Vatican II, Benedictines followed the Rule's pattern for the Divine Office, using Benedict's distribution of the Psalms and structure of the eight offices. However, the elaboration and enrichment of the Office with new liturgical texts and music (antiphons, hymns and responsories) made it longer and musically more demanding. Throughout the Middle Ages extra prayers and additional offices such as the Office of the Dead or of All Saints further lengthened the amount of time devoted to common prayer.

The practice of choral prayer also changed in significant ways. The pauses between the psalms for silent prayer were shortened and then eliminated. In Benedict's day the psalmody itself was chanted by a soloist while the choir responded with a refrain. By the time of the Carolingian reform, choral psalmody in which everyone sang the actual verses of the psalms, usually in alternation from side to side of the choir, had become standard. Liturgical psalmody seemed increasingly distinct from personal prayer and *lectio divina*.[3] Bernard of Monte Cassino wrote in the thirteenth century that 'in psalmody we speak to God; in *lectio* God speaks to us through the Scriptures. In the first we ask him about things; in the second, we understand the answer.'[4]

The expansion of the liturgy was already well under way early in the ninth century when Benedict of Aniane sought to impose the *Rule of Benedict* on the monasteries of Charlemagne's empire. The liturgical practices of this reform movement were based on the *Rule of Benedict*, but numerous elements were added to Benedict's framework. Most significant, as we shall see later, was the addition of a daily community Mass. The culmination of this process was the kind of elaborate liturgy associated most famously with the French abbey of Cluny. In such monasteries the choir monks or nuns would spend most of their time in church, leaving the manual work to lay brothers or sisters and to hired labour.[5]

Benedictine reform movements typically focus on the liturgy, whether to prune it back or to restore its integrity. The Cistercian reform of the twelfth century took aim at the Cluniac liturgical system in order to reclaim the balance of prayer and manual work prescribed by the *Rule*. Although the Cistercians saw themselves as returning to the ideal of the *Rule*, they in fact relied heavily on the work of both lay brothers and hired hands. The theological and liturgical ground had shifted so much from the sixth century that Benedict's original model was gone for good. Many monasteries in the late Middle Ages were faulted for neglecting or even abandoning the full round of daily offices.

The restored monasticism of Solesmes in nineteenth-century France tilted toward the ideal of Cluny, while the various primitive observance movements of the nineteenth and twentieth centuries were more Cistercian in their approach to the liturgy. Others respected the 'traditional' liturgical structures while adapting them to new circumstances. The timetable of the *Rule* was generally modified so that the office of Vigils was prayed later or even anticipated the evening before. In monasteries and congregations with schools and other external apostolates, offices were often combined or prayed at times which accommodated demands of work. Nineteenth-century American Benedictine women were actually sometimes forbidden by ecclesiastical authorities to pray the full Benedictine office lest it interfere with their works of service.[6] The reclaiming of the monastic office by many of these communities in the twentieth century was a landmark in their reassertion of monastic identity.

In most Benedictine monasteries on the eve of Vatican Council II, the community gathered fewer times than Benedict prescribed and prayed the office as quickly as possible simply to cover the liturgical ground. All of the appointed liturgical texts were duly sung and recited, though with less than the ideal contemplative attitude. Gregorian chant was loved by many but Latin was increasingly felt to increase the burden of the office. In male communities some of the choir monks began to envy the vernacular Divine Office of the lay brothers, which in the twentieth century came to replace the less liturgical forms of prayer which had previously been customary for the brothers.

The liturgical reforms after Vatican II dramatically changed both the form and the experience of Benedictine communal prayer. Given the opportunity to pray in the vernacular, the great majority of Benedictine communities throughout the world opted to pray in their own language and to develop appropriate musical forms. Benedict's permission to rearrange the distribution of Psalms (*RB* 18.22) was finally taken up, though his requirement that the full psalter be prayed weekly was generally set aside. Communities which had long since adopted a four- or five-fold pattern of daily prayer rationalized the offices to fit that pattern rather than combining them as had been done previously. The office of Prime disappeared; other day hours tended to be reduced in number; the office of Vigils was shortened or merged into either evening or morning prayer; Compline was sometimes relegated to private use.

In male monasteries the vernacular Divine Office meant that choir monks and lay brothers could pray together. Benedictine women assumed greater ownership of their liturgy, often experimenting with language and rituals expressive of their experience of Benedictine life. The men have typically been less adventurous. In most Benedictine monasteries today the liturgy is shorter, simpler, and quieter than it was decades ago. It is usually considered to be more prayerful, and certainly more accessible, than previously. No liturgical reform can resolve the perennial struggles with distraction, or salve annoyance with the less musically-gifted or the fidgety: in these respects modern Benedictines remain in experiential communion with their forebears. Surely additions and expansions will reshape the prayer of Benedictine communities in the future. If now the liturgy is a bit too spare for some tastes, another couple of hundred years of development and accretion will perhaps again bring cries for greater simplicity.

LECTIO DIVINA

Benedict expected his monks to spend up to three hours a day in *lectio*. Ancient reading was hard work, placing demands on both mind and body. It was done slowly and always vocalized, even if sotto voce.[7] Benedict knew that the monks of his monastery would find *lectio* difficult, and he even delegated seniors to ensure that their brothers really were using the time allotted for *lectio* rather than for entertainment or gossip (*RB* 48.17–20). If worse came to worst, Benedict conceded that the hopeless cases could be given some work to do so that they would not distract others by their restlessness (*RB* 48.17–23). During the Middle Ages, *lectio* was typically done in common, 'so that seeing one another they could encourage one another.'[8]

Although Benedict was clearly worried about misuse of time (his chapter on work and *lectio* begins with the maxim, 'idleness is the enemy of the soul', *RB* 48.1), the language he uses to describe time for *lectio* suggests more than filling up the horarium. The monks are to 'leave themselves free for' or 'give themselves over to' their reading.[9] *Lectio* is an opportunity for awareness of God's presence. Benedict's terminology recalls one of the earliest Latin rules. Written before technical vocabulary had developed very far, this rule simply says that the purpose of the first three hours of the day is *vacare Deo*, 'to be free for God'.[10] A thirteenth-century English customary urges the monks 'to love holy leisure (*otium sanctum*), during which time they undertake the business of their souls.'[11]

By Benedict's day, monastic legislators had become more specific about what time for God should involve. Benedict understands *lectio* to include both 'meditation' and reading (*RB* 48.23). He meant not the imaginative meditation introduced with the *devotio moderna* in the fourteenth century and found also in Jesuit spirituality, nor a mantra-based meditation, but the slow, prayerful recitation of biblical texts. This kind of meditation was linked to memorization, and *lectio* time provided the opportunity to commit the Bible to heart for use throughout the day and, especially, at the Work of God. In Benedict's days monks and nuns would not have had the luxury of a personal psalter or prayer book; memorizing the psalms for liturgical purposes was a necessity rather than an example of spiritual athleticism (*RB* 8.3, 48.13, 58.5). A thirteenth-century Benedictine urged his readers to remember each evening's common reading so that throughout the night,

whether desiring sleep or prayer, they would have something
to ruminate lest the devil find them at loose ends.[12]

Lent was a time of particular intensity for *lectio*, with an
extra hour given to it (*RB* 48.14). Chapter 49 of the *Rule*,
devoted entirely to Lenten observance, lists the spiritual practices of 'prayer with tears, reading, compunction of heart, and
self-denial'. During Lent each member of the community was
to be issued a book – most likely, a section of the Bible – to be
read 'straight through' (*RB* 48.15). Theodomar, Abbot of Monte
Cassino in the late eighth century, tells us that every monk
was also given a candle for Lent so that 'they might devote
themselves to sacred readings (*divinis lectionibus*) not only by
light of day but even at night.'[13]

Obviously the Bible was the staple of *lectio divina*. But it
was not the only book early Benedictines ever read. At Vigils
daily there were readings from early Christian commentaries
on the Bible. The reading at meals may have included non-
biblical works; it certainly has in later centuries. Each night
before Compline there was common spiritual reading which
could include Cassian's *Conferences* or other monastic and
theological literature (*RB* 42.3–7). At the end of the *Rule*,
Benedict provides a bibliography directing his readers to the
works of 'the holy Catholic Fathers', to Cassian's *Institutes*
and *Conferences*, to monastic hagiography and Basil's monastic
rules. Benedict's own acquaintance with Latin monastic and
theological literature included the standard texts.[14] He and
the monks of his monastery would have read such works
during their *lectio* periods or heard them during common
reading.

One monastery of the Carolingian reform summarized the
monastic programme for reading and meditation as: psalms,
canticles and hymns; the *Rule*; Scripture generally; commentaries on Scripture; the *Conferences* and *Lives* of the Fathers
(as in *RB* 73); grammatical arts and 'spiritual flowers', which
meant collections of favourite texts.[15] The same document
explains that the assigned time is to be used for 'entrusting
reading to memory.'[16] One readily sees the pre-eminence of

texts for liturgical preparation, prayerful meditation and understanding of the monastic life. The focus was conversion of heart rather than intellectual curiosity, though mind and heart obviously have to work together in the project of monastic living.

As the centuries passed, the concept and practice of *lectio* changed. The earlier broad view of *lectio*'s purpose and scope gradually narrowed. From being an inclusive way of describing the whole atmosphere of monastic mindfulness of God, *lectio* became more and more a discipline of 'spiritual reading', one among a variety of devotional practices.[17] Benedictines were influenced by new movements in the larger Church such as the *devotio moderna* of the fourteenth century with its emphasis on interior feelings and the practice of thematic meditation. There were also distinctive influences within the monastic world, like that of the post-Reformation English Benedictine Augustine Baker, who developed a form of meditative prayer inspired by the apophatic tradition of *The Cloud of Unknowing*. By the nineteenth and early twentieth centuries, Jesuit-style meditation and non-monastic spiritual manuals had become normal parts of monastic formation and staples of the spiritual life. A reductionist view of *lectio* prevailed.

The recent Benedictine 'return to the sources' has led to a rediscovery of the biblical basis and distinctive aspects of monastic *lectio*, allowing Benedictines once more to claim their own spiritual tradition and its way of praying the Bible. The abundance of books on *lectio*, many by non-monastic writers, testifies to the appeal of this simplest, though always challenging, practice of mindfulness of the presence of God in the Word. *Lectio* is sometimes presented as a method or technique of prayer, but it is really a kind of anti-technique, a disposition more than a method. Therefore it is hard to describe or teach because it varies so much from person to person, shaped by temperament, individual needs and ways of thinking.[18] Some people read slowly but steadily. Others ponder a word or phrase for the whole time. Others sweep the pages, trawling for morsels of nourishment. Much depends on the text being read, for some books of the Bible are denser in spiritual content than others.

Although the manner of doing *lectio* varies, the commitment to and centrality of *lectio* is a universal marker of Benedictine life. Fidelity to *lectio* is a daily reminder that we cannot bypass the Word. Listening in *lectio*, like listening at the Work of God, like listening to the *Rule* being read at table or in Chapter, like listening to a superior or a community member, deepens awareness of God's presence everywhere. Indeed, one's spiritual path can be retraced by reviewing the ways *lectio* has changed over the years, as it shaped and was being shaped by experience, growth in self-knowledge, increasing awareness of dependence upon the Word. Pressures of time and work, personal crises, periods of spiritual renewal can all be read in how (and how faithfully) one attends to *lectio*.

The various approaches to *lectio* converge when it comes to the basics. Because *lectio* is a challenging discipline it demands regularity and focus. Benedict gave the best hours of the day (in the forenoon) to *lectio*. Most people find that they need to establish a set time each day given over to *lectio* and nothing else. Many monasteries provide a period for *lectio* in the common schedule; whether there is an assigned time or not, it still remains up to each person to be faithful to the practice. The experience of most people is that *lectio* works best at the start of the day or at the end so that it does not have to compete for mental and emotional space with everything else. Having a regular place for *lectio* also helps to consecrate that part of the day. It is not surprising that time and place, the key elements of Benedictine stability, are the keys to *lectio*.

Modern Benedictines find Benedict's prescription of two to three hours of *lectio* per day to be more than they can manage. Whether or not they are involved in apostolates external to the monastery, nuns and monks today typically work too hard and too long to devote that much time to a spiritual exercise that demands concentration and energy. Part of the difference is that Benedict's *lectio* included more of what we would label 'study' and do at another time. In modern practice, about half an hour seems a starting point for prayerful immersion in a text. Many people find that their desire and need for more time devoted to *lectio* increases with age and experience.

For some Benedictines reading the Bible and biblically-based spiritual works is welcome intellectual stimulation, while for others *lectio* is a break from highly intellectual work of other kinds. In either case, *lectio* today is usually distinguished from study directed toward a particular goal or accomplishment. *Lectio* does not rush toward a deadline or a product. Most practitioners of *lectio* feel a need to learn more about the history and theology of the Bible, and the interplay of such preparatory study and actual encounter with the biblical text becomes a matter for discernment lest *lectio* time be entirely usurped by study which appeals to the head at the expense of the heart.

Lectio is meant to be a conversation with God about one's life. To foster that conversation, some people employ structured exercises of reflection on their reading or take notes. Others find *lectio* time valuable precisely because it is not structured. They find their *lectio* of the Bible flowing naturally into *lectio* of life or of natural beauty. A philosopher asked Antony the Great, 'How do you manage without the consolation of books?' Antony replied, 'My book is the nature of created things, and it is there whenever I want to read the words of God.'[19]

The experience of *lectio divina* today is impaired by the decline of the art of reading. Both skimming and speed-reading are antithetical to *lectio divina*. Perhaps even more subversive has been the loss of the biblical consciousness which was natural to Benedict and his medieval successors. Their principal source of stories, imagery and intellectual stimulation was the Bible. Scripture helped to create the world they inhabited and was the key to interpreting it.[20] The other books they read were expositions of biblical themes or aids to interpreting the Bible itself. This is no longer true. The challenge now is keeping a mental grip on the biblical words heard or read in the course of days flooded with other kinds of verbiage and imagery.

BENEDICTINES AND LEARNING

Benedictines are traditionally identified with scholarship as well as liturgy. This stereotype is only partly accurate. Because Benedict legislates for child oblation, we know that his monks raised and educated children within the monastery. There is no question that after his day intellectual work became increasingly prominent in monasteries. Part of the impetus was entirely pragmatic: Benedictines had to be taught how to read and what to read. The literacy of newcomers to the monastery could by no means be presumed, and even the literate required guidance in biblical, spiritual and theological subjects.[21] In western monastic life until very recently, Latin was the key to theological literacy and the study of Latin grammar had to be emphasized for educational purposes.[22] Sometimes children from outside were taught also, though in the Middle Ages there was a strong bias against running external schools.

The sources from which Benedict drew in writing his *Rule* display an ambivalence toward learning that runs throughout western monastic history. Early monastic writers protest the dangers of study for its own sake and are distinctly uncomfortable about the role of pre-Christian classical literature in monastic intellectual formation. Jerome's nightmare in which he was accused before the judgement seat of God of being a Ciceronian rather than a Christian is the most vivid example of a tension found in many other monastic texts.[23] None the less, the copying of manuscripts and the composition of original works of theology, biblical commentary or natural science developed naturally from Benedict's emphasis on *lectio*. Inevitably, some found themselves drawn more and more deeply into the texts they read, and were inspired to contribute to the tradition they had received.

Intellectual work suited monastic stability and could be

readily fitted to the horarium. Social factors also played a role. In the highly class-conscious society of the Middle Ages, those from more privileged backgrounds were disinclined toward manual work. In response to the danger of social elitism one of the recurring themes of monastic reform has been the importance of manual labour for everyone in the community. Medieval monastic culture, as it evolved in the direction most fully exemplified by Cluny, also placed greater and greater intellectual demands on those who devised and practised the liturgy. Commentaries on the liturgy became staple monastic texts, joining the numerous early Christian and medieval biblical commentaries. Whatever form monastic writing of the Middle Ages took, whether discourse (as in Rupert of Deutz, twelfth century), poetic and dramatic (the Saxon canoness Hrosvit, tenth century), or visionary (Hildegard of Bingen, twelfth century, or Gertrude the Great, thirteenth century), it tended to stay close to the Bible and the liturgy, and to be concerned primarily with growth in the spiritual life.

Monastic theologians were often uneasy with the rise of the Schools in major cities during the twelfth century. That different kind of theological exploration, more analytical and speculative, shifted the centre of gravity of Latin theology from *lectio divina* to academic disputation. Although still informed by faith and the practice of the spiritual life, such theology was none the less different in tone and emphasis from the earlier monastic approach.

The difference between the traditional monastic and the scholastic methods can be seen in their handling of sources. The monastic writers, to the frustration of later editors and students, rarely cited their sources. It is not always clear that there was a source. The ideas gleaned in *lectio* and ruminated over and over became so smoothly woven into the writer's thought that trying to pick apart the threads can be difficult or even impossible. In the work of Thomas Aquinas, in contrast, literary sources are used in a way closer to that of modern academic writing, as authorities to be deployed – and duly cited – in order to bolster the argument being presented.

To be sure, the precursors of scholasticism can be found among monastic theological writings. Anselm's essays in speculative theology and the florilegia of favourite texts helped to prepare the way for later medieval methods, whether of Abelard, Peter Lombard or Thomas Aquinas. After the twelfth century, however, and its extraordinary flowering of spiritual theology among the Cistercians, the centrality of monastic theology to the western Church ended. Benedictines more and more found their way into the Schools. By the fourteenth century, both Benedictine and Cistercian male communities were even required to send a certain percentage of young monks off to houses of study at the major universities.[24]

The place of scholarship in monastic life has never been fully resolved. It was never the case that most Benedictines were scholars. In the twelfth century Abelard complained about the neglect of reading,[25] and in the late medieval period the low standard of literacy, much less intellectual life, was often the subject of visitation reports. The Congregation of St-Maur in the seventeenth and eighteenth centuries represented a unique concentration of monastic scholarship but its number of active scholars was never more than a small fraction of its membership.[26] The reform of the Cistercians led by Armand-Jean de Rancé of La Trappe in the late seventeenth century was a reaction at least in part against what Rancé perceived to be the effeteness of the Maurist emphasis on scholarship. Rancé counselled another abbot against allowing his monks to study philosophy: 'You will dry up their hearts, through study you will take away the spirit of prayer, you will put them off manual work.'[27] The accusation is inevitably reminiscent of the stance of the early Cistercians against the Cluniac total emphasis on liturgy.

The great Maurist Jean Mabillon defended the legitimacy of monastic scholarship (as well as of manual labour) in his remarkable *Treatise on Monastic Studies*.[28] Despite a personal reconciliation between the disputants the issue itself is a perennial matter of discernment. Even Benedictines harbour a suspicion of 'intellectual pride', which is perhaps a more likely temptation for some of them than the 'spiritual pride' to which those of stricter religious orders may be susceptible. The question is always one of goal and end: study, like any form of work, can become an end in itself and thereby an escape from the real focus of monastic life, the growth in charity that Benedict calls *conversatio morum.*

Despite the Maurists and subsequent bursts of monastic scholarship (generally French), in recent centuries monastic theologians have played a major role only in the emergence of the twentieth-century liturgical movement and the emphasis on 'return to the sources' of early Christian theology.[29] Monastic scholarship tended to remain historical and textual rather than philosophical or doctrinal. One now finds the Benedictine contribution to theological scholarship to be diminishing, partly because of declining numbers and partly because of the demands of other kinds of work. It is to be hoped that the monastic voice will not be lost from scholarly conversations. What does continue to emerge from monasteries is good spiritual theology, generally on a popular level.[30] The very possibility of distinguishing 'spiritual theology' from other kinds of theology, of course, is alien to the monastic tradition. Part of monastic work in the years to come may be to help in their reintegration.

EUCHARIST

There is no explicit reference in Benedict's liturgical code (*RB* 2.8–20) to the celebration of the Eucharist. The Eucharist was not an exclusively monastic practice and perhaps he simply saw no need to write about it – very few early monastic writers did. Almost certainly there was not a daily celebration of the Eucharist in Benedict's monastery. His monks probably received communion daily from the reserved sacrament, as did the monks in the Master's monastery.[31] On Sundays they may have gone to the parish church as did the Master's monks, though Benedict's allowance of clerics in the monastery (*RB*

60 and 62) suggests that the monks probably did have their own Sunday celebration.

Evidently Benedict himself was not a priest, and the expectation that the abbots of male monasteries would be priests still lay in the future when he wrote his *Rule*. None the less, the *Rule* reflects a time when monasticism and clerical life were beginning the entanglement that would lead to the two-class system of choir monks and lay brothers which structured male monastic life from the Middle Ages until Vatican II.[32] Benedict, unlike the Master, allows priests to join the monastery (*RB* 60) and also foresees that the abbot may wish to have one of the monks ordained (*RB* 62). Both were wary of clerics because of possible challenges to the absolute authority of the abbot, though both also indicate great respect for the priesthood. They were formed by a tradition which saw monasticism and the clerical state as distinct ways of life in the Church. They could co-exist only in someone who had a very clear sense of obedience to the abbot and the *Rule*.

The evolution of eucharistic practice and theology in the larger Church soon led to daily celebration of the Eucharist in monastic communities. The practice of offering Masses for the dead and for various other intentions combined to increase the number of priests in monasteries of men. Monasteries of women depended on a chaplain, often a monk from a nearby community, for the daily Mass and other sacramental ministry. In male communities increasingly there were 'private' Masses as well, celebrated by each priest at the numerous side altars in the monastic church. The balance of Divine Office and eucharistic liturgy was significantly different from that envisaged by Benedict. The first controversy over the manner of the eucharistic presence of Christ was conducted by two monks of Corbie, Paschasius Radbertus and Ratramnus, in the ninth century. Ever since, monastic writers have been producing works of eucharistic theology and piety.

In Benedictine life before Vatican II the eucharistic practice in male communities included a 'conventual' or community Mass at which none but the celebrant received communion, as well as 'private' Masses served by lay brothers or junior monks. All monk-priests, who almost always constituted the majority of the community, were expected to celebrate the Eucharist daily. In communities of women the daily conventual Mass celebrated by their chaplain had pride of place in the horarium.

With Vatican II the advent of concelebration meant a great reduction in the number of 'private' Masses and the celebration of a single daily conventual Mass at which all could receive communion. In some male communities there has been a decline in the number of monks seeking ordination as the monastic and clerical roles have become more clearly distinguished, though other communities have become actually more clerical in character. Although Benedictine women still depend on chaplains for Eucharist and sacramental celebrations, an often painful reminder of the exclusion of women from ordained ministry in the Roman Catholic Church, they have maintained a non-clerical monasticism long impossible for men.

PERSONAL PRAYER

Whatever form of personal prayer Benedictines choose, it is always to be grounded in the reality of the self embraced by a merciful God. The hints Gregory the Great provides of Benedict's own experience of prayer suggest that with such grounding he was able to see the transfiguration of all things by the loving light of God. Whether Gregory gives us Benedict's actual experience or not, he describes an atmosphere of prayer traditionally monastic and certainly familiar to Benedict.

Benedict tells us little about the non-liturgical prayer of his monks. He acknowledges that monks will want to make use of the monastic oratory for personal prayer, whether immediately following the common offices or at other times; such prayer should be quiet (lest it disturb others), tearful and focused (*RB* 52.4). An eighth-century customary from Monte Cassino, for example, foresees that some may wish to pray privately in the oratory after the main meal of the day, and notes that the liturgical regulations about when kneeling is permitted do not apply to private prayer, for which kneeling is always an option for those who wish.[33] Benedict mentions that his monks will pray for one another, for those undertaking community tasks, for those in trouble, for and with guests.[34]

The interplay of the Work of God, *lectio divina* and personal prayer has always been complex and resistant to categories or distinctions. All of these aspects of prayer are united in cultivation of awareness of the presence of God. The medieval monks of Eynsham, near Oxford, were reminded: 'After Vespers or supper, what could be more fitting or sweeter than to go into the cloister, and to use that time to read or to pray or to recollect what one did or said or thought during the day, giving heartfelt thanks for the good, and asking forgiveness for sins and negligence?'[35] To read, to pray, to place oneself before God: the flow from one to the other is meant to be entirely natural.

Benedict tells us nothing about the kinds or forms of prayer he and his monks practised. They knew the tradition of mono-logistic prayer brought to the west by John Cassian in which one chooses a biblical phrase or brief petition and repeats it over and over until it becomes a prayerful undercurrent to both day and night, sometimes rising to explicit awareness as a conscious form of prayer.[36] Cassian had recommended the use of the opening lines of Psalm 70, 'God, come to my assistance: Lord, make haste to help me', which Benedict used as the opening versicles of the day hours of the Divine Office. He and his first readers knew their Cassian, and the point of this coincidence would not have been lost on them. Personal prayer and common prayer were different moments in the one great experience of communion with God. In his twelfth degree of humility (*RB* 7.62–6), Benedict describes someone who has completely internalized the virtue of awareness of God. As if already standing before the judgement seat of God, such a person constantly says in the heart the prayer of the tax collector from Luke 18:13: 'Lord, I am a sinner, not worthy to look up to heaven.' Both Benedict's emphasis on continual prayer in the heart (cf. *RB* 7.11) and his choice of this text unite him with the great eastern tradition of unceasing prayer which flowered in the practice and teaching of the Jesus Prayer.[37]

Whenever Benedict wrote about the experience of prayer, he wrote about tears.[38] For this approach we must again look to the eastern monastic traditions mediated to the Latin west largely by John Cassian. The theme of *penthos* ('repentant sorrow'), often translated into Latin as *compunctio*, was the eastern analogue of Benedict's humility and always had a special link to prayer. Like humility, *penthos* was to be the mark of both the novice and the elder. With growth in humility came ever-deeper awareness of one's own sinfulness, as well as compassion and tears for the sins of other people. Such mindfulness meant deep feeling, and deep feeling meant tears. This was not overwrought pathos, for the tears of sorrow were mingled with tears of joy celebrating the forgiveness secured in Christ. A monastic Christian is like the Prodigal Son at the festive meal, keenly aware of failure and irresponsibility, overwhelmed by a love that not only receives back but celebrates the return.

Benedict's emphasis on a physical descriptor of prayer such as tears may surprise the modern western reader accustomed to more sublimated forms of spiritual practice. In fact, tears pervade the early monastic literature.[39] One great monk was said to have wept off his eyelashes and worn a groove in his chest from all of his weeping.[40] Tears were often described as the bread of the monastic life. The very language of compunction was graphically physical. Both the Latin word *compunctio* and its Greek ancestor, *katanyxis*, denote pricking or goading, here applied to the heart. Puncture a human heart and it will bleed; pierce it spiritually and the result is tears. Ancient people knew the therapeutic value of tears that modern science has rediscovered. Like the waters of baptism, tears cleanse and heal. They purify the heart, and the pure of heart can see God (Matt. 5:8). As physical manifestations of deep emotion, tears engage the body in the work of the spirit. Indeed, tears of the saints (and of Christ himself) were considered precious relics and vivid signs of holiness. In urging his monks to weep, Benedict is not recommending dramatic or unusual behaviour. He is simply telling them to pray with awareness, and awareness will bring tears. Purity of heart, tears of compunction, intention of heart: these simple but deeply traditional synonyms for prayerful awareness of God shape Benedictine prayer.

Benedictines have also used the devotional practices brought to them through developments in the larger Church. One thinks particularly of the rosary and other Marian devotions, 'mental prayer', imaginative meditations, novenas, etc. Today many also find the Jesus Prayer, centring prayer or other simple meditative practices to be particularly complementary to *lectio divina* and the Divine Office. Because Christian meditation is always rooted in the Word, the principle of biblical emphasis arguably should guide the choice of a phrase used for meditative prayer. In this sense Christian monastic meditation is distinctive when compared to forms of mantra-based meditation in which the repeated phrase is meant to be devoid of content. Cassian describes his brief phrase from the Psalms as a way into the rest of the Bible, a link between personal prayer, *lectio*, and the Liturgy of the Hours.

SILENCE

Benedict was pragmatic about the need for quiet in his monastery. His monks were together almost all of the time during the day and slept in the same room at night. With no private rooms in which to find solitude and silence, whatever quiet there was had to be found in common spaces. Taciturnity was necessary lubrication for community life, preserving peace and fostering prayer. Therefore Benedict's sharpest injunctions about silence apply when noise would have been most disruptive: during the (unamplified!) table reading in the refectory, at night, in the dormitory and oratory.[41]

Besides when and where to be silent, there is the more

fundamental issue of how to speak. Benedict advises that speech be rare, brief and simple. His chapter on silence (*RB* 6) teaches by its length rather than its content, for Benedict has reduced the Master's two prolix and almost incoherent chapters, totalling eighty-eight verses, to a single chapter of eight verses.[42] The result is severe and primarily ascetical in tone. Uncontrolled speech is dangerous; even good words are risky. Community members should not speak unless spoken to. Attitude counts for everything. Trashy talk is never acceptable, nor is gossip.[43]

There is practical wisdom in such advice, but not the spiritual depth we would hope for. Benedict never writes of mystical silence except to remind us that our purity of heart and tears of *compunctio* move God more than our words (*RB* 20.3–4). His teaching on the manner of speech, however, does place the use of language firmly in the context of the pervasive virtue of humility. Benedict follows the Master in requiring that all speech be offered humbly, i.e., directly and simply. He innovates by adding 'reasonably' in several passages.[44] The issue becomes more clearly one of stewardship. Language is a gift that can be used thoughtfully or thoughtlessly, humbly or proudly. Someone constantly aware of the presence of God will know when and how to speak.

Benedictines today have far more privacy than did Benedict's monks. Private rooms are the norm, work is often solitary, there is more free time in the schedule. The purely pragmatic imperative for taciturnity is less acute. The issue of quiet, however, endures. Along with greater opportunity for silence has come the introduction of more kinds of noise via radios, television and other audio-visual media. Learning to distinguish conversation that upbuilds and strengthens from malicious and destructive gossip has an analogue in discerning when news or music or TV programmes are informative and inspiring or distracting and even destructive. The irony is that both noise and silence can become defences against painful truths. Sound can banish the quiet which threatens to confront us with the truth of ourselves. Silence, equally, can be used as

a cocoon protecting us against those people who would challenge us or make demands we are unprepared to meet. Silence
can also become a weapon, wielded in icy ignoring of others
even for years at a time. Both compulsive chattiness and sullen
silence miss the Benedictine mark of attentive listening and
reverent reply.

3. OBEDIENCE AND HUMILITY

STANDING BEFORE GOD AND HUMANKIND

For Benedict, as for the whole tradition before him, the key to monastic life was accountability to God and to other people. Accountability galvanizes community, marking the difference between mere cohabitation and genuinely common purpose. In more solitary forms of monasticism, accountability is concretized in a relationship to a spiritual elder. In cenobitic life this obedience extends beyond the superior to a communal rule of life and to the other members of the community.

When Benedict describes monastic community, he contrasts it not to the life of the hermit but of those who call themselves monks but live independently (the Sarabaites of *RB* 1.6–9). Whether they live alone or with other people, such pseudo-monks listen only to themselves: 'their law is what they like to do, whatever strikes their fancy. Anything they believe in and choose, they call holy. Anything they dislike, they consider forbidden' (*RB* 1.8–9). They are frauds because they are entirely self-centred. The genuine hermit, who has become self-reliant with respect to human community, remains completely reliant on the help of God.

As Benedict sees it, such total dependence on God rather than on one's own desires and preferences develops best in community. Even hermits have been 'long-tested in the monastery' before undertaking a life of solitude (*RB* 1.3). Thus 'hermit' is not the antonym of 'cenobite', but its occasional variant. According to Gregory, Benedict himself had taken the opposite path, beginning in solitude and ending up in community. From the hints we explored earlier, the trajectory was not a smooth one. The best kind of self-awareness, the kind leading to deeper and deeper awareness of God, occurs in the company of others. For most people, to become truly individual before God requires immersion in the common life.

OBEDIENCE

What is the point of accountability, of this virtue of 'obedience'? At the most basic level, obedience acknowledges and rejects the futility of isolation. Left entirely to ourselves we can do little but despair. Opening ourselves to God's refashioning work opens the possibility of the life given to us by Christ's obedience. As the wise abbess in Iris Murdoch's novel *The Bell* reminds us, 'the way is always forward, never back.' The way forward, for Benedict, meant obedience. As part of the very first sentence of the *Rule*, he writes: 'by the labor of obedience you will return to the one from whom you retreated by the laziness of disobedience' (*RB* Prol. 2).

The hard work of obedience happens in relationships. Obedience consists of a word spoken and heard: the Latin word behind 'obedience' means 'listening'. Obedience is thus essentially a conversation, an intimate exchange based upon trust that the relationship is life-giving. The fundamental conversation is that between each human person and God. The word is spoken through the Bible and in prayer. Monastic life is based upon the Christian recognition that God's word to each of us can be mediated in human relationships as well, provided that they are grounded in attentive listening and prayer.

Monastic obedience is a complex and sometimes fragile dynamic. It works most smoothly when it is impersonal, a matter of following a community policy. It has its greatest effect, however, when it involves discernment on a personal level. The word given and heard may be a work assignment, or an invitation to deeper fidelity after failure, or a challenge to complacency. Obedience is vitiated by mistrust or abuse, though the more common barrier is lack of trust, the unwillingness to listen no matter how trustworthy the 'other', whether divine or human, may be. This is why early monastic writers emphasize obedience strongly and even absolutely. Their rigour should not be confused with so-called 'blind' obedience: the concern was to jolt their readers out of another kind of blindness, that of inattentiveness or disobedience. Benedict describes it as waking up: 'let us open our eyes to the divine light, and let us listen attentively to the divine voice which calls out daily, warning us: "If today you hear his voice, harden not your hearts" (Ps. 95:8)' (*RB* Prol. 9). For obedience to work, all of the parties must be awake. The superior has to be every bit as obedient as the members of the community. All alike stand before God and under the authority of the *Rule*.[1]

Benedict presents his teaching on obedience in the opening and closing sections of the *Rule*. In the Prologue and the early chapters, he emphasizes the individual and 'vertical' dimensions of obedience, as one is obedient to God and to the superior. The essence of such obedience is Christological. Five of the six scriptural quotations in Benedict's chapter 'On Obedience' (*RB* 5) are from the New Testament. The most important of them is John 6:38, which recurs in the chapter 'On Humility': 'I have come not to do my own will, but the will of him who sent me' (*RB* 5.13, 7.32). By living in a monastery under a spiritual mother or father, Benedict claims, cenobites imitate that obedience of Christ. The monastic superior speaks with divine authority. The disciple, like Christ, lays aside all that pertains to self in order to be totally open to the word offered (*RB* 5.4,7,15).

Benedict's is an austere ideal, truly a 'narrow way' (*RB* 5.11). Although it is theologically sound, it needs humanizing, conditioning it to the realities of human frailty. The conditioner is no less theological, but for that no less human. Love must be the driving force, the kind of love that 'holds Christ more precious than all else' (*RB* 5.2,10). Without love, obedience is impossible: Christ, after all, was a beloved son, not a masochist. Given such love, obedience becomes natural. While love is taking root, however, obedience is vulnerable to the corrosive effects of self-protection and protracted by interludes of calculation.

Benedict assures us that it gets easier. The Prologue to the *Rule* is filled with images of 'running', used to strengthen the imperative tone of the divine call. With progress in the monastic life and in faith, we 'run the path of the command-ments, the heart expanding with the inexpressible sweetness of love' (*RB* Prol. 49). The cardiovascular image is deliberate, for monastic obedience is a lifetime's training programme that builds up heart, soul, mind and body. The result is someone who 'always manifests humility not only in the heart but even in the body itself: at the Work of God, in the oratory, in the monastery, in the garden, on the road, in the field or anywhere else' (*RB* 7.62–3). In that description of perfect humility we see the result of perfect obedience. Benedict's humility is the companion and fruit of obedience, the mode of being of someone who hears and takes to heart every reminder of dependence on God alone.

HUMILITY

Benedict's chapter on humility is the longest of the *Rule* and in many ways its heart. He describes humility with the meta-phor of a ladder. By its twelve steps of humility in the present life, one ascends to heaven. The ladder image is more arresting than cogent. Apart from the first and the twelfth steps there is no evident progression among them. In fact, when the chap-ters on obedience and humility are compared, one finds two different first steps of humility: unhesitating obedience (*RB* 5.1) and never forgetting the fear of God (*RB* 7.10). At least six of the steps of humility (nos. 2–6,8) are actually aspects of monastic obedience and three are about restraint of speech (nos. 9–11). The chapter on humility in effect recapitulates the two previous chapters on obedience and silence. It becomes impossible to disentangle humility from obedience, and the proper use of speech pertains to both. We shall see a similar problem in the Benedictine vow formula, which employs three more or less synonymous terms to describe monastic life.

Benedict tells us that the first step of humility is 'fear of God' (*RB* 7.10). This biblical term describes the fundamental Christian reality check, a recognition of that presence of God so palpable to Benedict. The emphasis here is on God's awareness of human thoughts and actions. If God is vigilant, so must we be. The second and third steps stake out the basis of monastic obedience, the laying aside of self-will and submission to a superior. The fourth to sixth play out the practical consequences: the inevitability of painful trials, the need to be open with one's superior about failures, giving up the expectation of special treatment. To these we must add the eighth, which limits the range of behaviour to the norms of the monastery's rule and the example of the superiors.

The seventh step of humility is the most wrenching for modern readers: 'that one not only claims with the tongue to be inferior and worse than everyone else, but actually believes it with deep feeling of heart' (*RB* 7.51). The kick comes in the succeeding words, borrowed from Psalm 22: 'humbling oneself and saying with the prophet, "I am a worm and not a human being, cursed by others and rejected by the people." ' Ask a first-time reader of the *Rule* what is most distasteful and this is likely to head the list. The key, as so often in the *Rule*, lies in tracking the biblical quotations which follow: 'I was exalted but now I am humbled and confused' (Ps. 88:16, Latin) and 'it is good that you have humbled me, so that I could learn your commandments' (Ps. 119:71). Here we have the entire trajectory of monastic compunction: from false sense of self (exalted) to painful self-recognition (helpless, confused), which is the only place where listening to God can happen (learning your commandments).

The language is harsh, cutting through the promises of self-actualization valued in modern western culture. Opposite to the message preached by apostles of self-esteem, these words are indeed dangerous. With their power to cut through layers of self-protection, they are capable of misuse by oneself or by those intent on oppression. Within Benedict's context of God's abiding presence, however, these are words of liberation, not of oppression. They promise freedom from the burden of creating and maintaining a (false) public image. They invite the fearful self behind the mask to hear a new voice.

Benedict's twelfth step of humility contains the description quoted above of the person who manifests humility always and everywhere. Heart and body are completely at one. Such a person, Benedict claims, stands as if already at the final judgement, fully aware of a lifetime of sin and infidelity. But that is not the complete story. The full insight is that taught to such great effect by Martin Luther a thousand years later: the Christian is *simul iustus et peccator*, a sinner indeed but redeemed by the infinite mercy of God in Christ. When it has been fully realized, Benedict claims, humility is incompatible with fear, for the fruit of humility is the 'perfect love of God which casts out fear' (1 Jn 4:18 as in *RB* 7.67). Fear of God is transformed into love, which casts out all other fears.

Thus Benedict concludes the first part of the *Rule*, as he did the Prologue, with the reassurance that practice makes perfect. The labour of obedience has become natural, a good habit founded upon delight in virtue. The God whose presence was recognized at the outset has accomplished this great work through the Holy Spirit (*RB* 7.70).

MUTUAL OBEDIENCE

Benedict revisits the theme of obedience in the final section of the *Rule*. There he gives us his own reflections, unmediated by the *Rule of the Master* which had been the basis of the chapters on obedience and humility earlier on. By introducing a concept of 'mutual obedience', Benedict tempers the more exclusively hierarchical approach of his predecessors and opens the way for modern focus on monastic community. Traditional commentaries on the *Rule* have often tended to read it prospectively rather than retrospectively, emphasizing the first seven chapters and reading the rest of the *Rule* in that light.

Commentators today increasingly emphasize the opposite approach, using chapters 71–2 as the interpretative key to the earlier sections of the *Rule*. Because Benedict speaks in his own voice here, rather than with the Master's, this approach has much to commend it.[2] The ninth-century commentary of Hildemar simply notes that Benedict ends the *Rule* in breadth of obedience and charity, perfecting the virtues in which he had begun.[3]

The principle is simple: 'the good of obedience should be shown by all, but not just to the superior: for they should obey one another, knowing that it is by this way of obedience that they go to God' (*RB* 71.1–2). The immediate application remains hierarchical, though it extends throughout the community as each person obeys all those who are senior. In the next chapter, however, Benedict levels the relationship completely. This chapter on 'Good Zeal' (*RB* 72) summarizes Benedict's teaching in a brief but deeply moving series of maxims. Obedience becomes fully mutual as the members of the community act with 'most fervent love', vying to show their respect for one another, to bear one another's weaknesses of mind and body, to be obedient to one another, to prefer to benefit others rather than oneself. The whole *Rule* is epitomized in the chapter's final words: 'let them offer the love of brother or sister selflessly to one another. Let them fear God lovingly, love their superior with sincere and humble love, prefer nothing whatsoever to Christ; and may he bring us together to everlasting life' (*RB* 72.8–12).

Benedict does not wait until the very end of the *Rule* to introduce the theme of attentiveness to one another in community. Early on he allows for consultation with the community (*RB* 3). In his chapter on the dormitory he urges the monks to encourage one another to arise for the Work of God and to undertake a seemly competition to get there first (*RB* 22.6,8). We have already seen his conviction of the presence of Christ in the other which drives service of the sick and the guest. In community the motivation is simpler: 'they should serve one another ... for by [service] one obtains greater reward and love' (*RB* 35.1–2; cf. 36.5). Serving others for the sake of a reward strikes us as distastefully mercenary, but for Benedict the reward was heavenly, not temporal: like all of the monastic life, practical care of other people advances one along the road to eternal life.

ORDER IN COMMUNITY

Benedict's most ample treatment of communal dynamics comes in his prescriptions about excommunication and rank. Both are problematic subjects today. Benedict's system of punishment for offences against the *Rule* arises from a psychology and culture different from that of most modern readers of the *Rule*, and his emphasis on rank strikes many readers, especially perhaps the North Americans, as rather *ancien régime*. Both topics, however, are very important to him and occupy significant portions of the *Rule*: twelve chapters are on faults and excommunication (*RB* 23–30, 43–6) and four touch on aspects of rank (*RB* 60–3). Even though in practice these subjects may no longer bear the significance they did for Benedict, they allow us to see how he put his theological principles into action. To bring his teaching on excommunication home, we can add to it his concern, indeed his fixation, on the vice of murmuring, that acid of complaining which eats away the fabric of community life. While excommunication and rank may not seem directly applicable today, murmuring has lost none of its destructive potency. Looking at all three can contribute to asking questions about what Benedictine obedience means in present practice.

Excommunication and Reconciliation

Benedict followed his predecessors in establishing procedures for handling infractions of monastic discipline. The tone is patient and just. Private warnings precede public ones and excommunication is a last resort. Punishment must correspond to the gravity of the fault. Corporal punishment is reserved for those unable to understand the more subtle penalties (*RB* 23–4). If one remembers the social and cultural context of Benedict's *Rule*, his approach is comparatively enlightened.

Our particular interest lies with Benedict's sanction of excommunication. It begins with exclusion from common table, which means eating later and alone, and is linked to the oratory in that the excommunicated cannot exercise the liturgical ministries of cantor or reader. A more serious form would extend to banishment from the oratory entirely and assignment of solitary forms of work. Throughout this period none of the community are to speak with the one who has been excommunicated. Human contact rests with the abbot, who is to be deeply involved with every aspect of the case, and the abbot's delegates. Benedict calls these agents *senpectae*, a word of uncertain derivation but with a clear meaning: these pastoral trouble-shooters can work where the superior cannot. Benedict appreciated that oftentimes an authority figure is the least able to effect progress in a difficult instance. The superior's role will concern us more elsewhere. Here we note the extension of spiritual authority beyond the superior. The last resort in obstinate cases is to involve the whole community in prayer, turning everything over to God's care after all human remedies have been exhausted (*RB* 28.4–5). Obviously prayer has accompanied the process from the beginning, and the community knew who was excommunicated by absence from table and oratory. Benedict may have in mind a special kind of prayer or simply be noting that human efforts can take things only so far.

In Benedict's monastery the ritual of reconciliation of the excommunicated is similarly communal. The most serious case, excommunication from table and oratory, requires prostration in silence outside the door of the oratory at the end of the Work of God. This powerful symbol of desire for reconciliation is offered to the members of the community as they file past their brother on their way to common table or work. When the abbot determines that the next stage is appropriate, the penitent prostrates at the feet of each monk, beginning with the abbot. Probably occurring inside the oratory, the practice re-enacts the ritual of admission to the community at monastic profession (*RB* 44.4, cf. *RB* 58.23). At this point the abbot can readmit him to the choir, in whatever place he decides, though he still cannot exercise a liturgical role and must prostrate in his place at the end of each hour of the Work of God until the abbot determines that the process of reconciliation is complete. Those excommunicated from only the common table perform the prostrations at their place in the oratory.

Other, less grave, faults have a similarly public penalty attached to them. Latecomers to the oratory are to stand apart for the duration of the office and then to 'make satisfaction', i.e., to prostrate at the end of it. Those who arrive late for meals or leave early must eat separately (and without wine!) if they do so more than twice (*RB* 43.13–17). Mistakes in the liturgy are to be acknowledged by a prostration then and there (*RB* 45.1); mistakes at work are to be similarly acknowledged (*RB* 46.1–4).

Benedict prescribed these rituals for public and objective transgressions. The point was not thought-control or abusive manipulation of conscience by airing someone's innermost sins. Private matters are to be revealed only to the superior or one of the 'spiritual elders' (*RB* 46.5, another instance of delegated spiritual authority). The point was both to obtain healing and to preserve appropriate privacy, for these people 'know how to cure their own wounds as well as those of others, without exposing and publicizing them' (*RB* 46.6). The significance and practice of such spiritual counsel will concern us later. Here we note that obedience – and failures of obedience – had communal, public aspects considered by Benedict to be central to the monastic life.

There are few monastic communities today which practise anything like Benedict's policies of excommunication. Many have preserved some form of 'chapter of faults' in which short-comings can be admitted and forgiveness sought; 'kneeling out' when late to common prayer or table is not uncommon. It is clear that Benedict envisaged something more robust and fundamental. Recovering that spirit is difficult, and not helped in western countries by the shift in consciousness which has made autonomy, rather than community, the default mode.

Absence from table and oratory, which for Benedict was a punishment, has become a privilege and even a 'right' arrogated for a variety of reasons ranging from psychological self-protection to demands of work to personal preference and sheer inertia. Anyone who lives in a monastic community knows how hard it can be to face the same people several times daily for a lifetime. It sometimes happens that a certain distance, a self-imposed excommunication, can become necessary for a time when sorting through questions of purpose and commitment. The return of a community member from either internal or external exile is a joyous event, though rarely celebrated openly.

The fact that some remain on the margins for the long term is one of the most complex and disturbing elements of community life, especially to the young who have come to the monastery precisely for the support of seeking God in community. The key question is not 'why does so-and-so not do X?', for the person in question may not really know why. Rather, the issue again is accountability. What are the links between so-and-so and the superiors, with a spiritual elder, with friends in the monastery? If the external practice is not ideal, how are the internal issues of intention and vocation kept alive?

The kind of silent tolerance that keeps bad marriages going far too long, or salvageable marriages out of the dry dock which could repair and relaunch them, is what Benedict sought to avoid through his teaching on obedience. He reminds us that making a collection of characters into a community requires hard work and inevitably entails some degree of failure. The test of community is whether – and how – its members acknowledge and deal with the cracks in its fabric.

Murmuring

Benedict abandons his normally moderate tone when writing about the vice of 'murmuring'. Endemic to organizations and communities of every kind, this resistant or whiny attitude creates black holes of negativity. Departing from his usual conciseness vis-à-vis the *Rule of the Master*, Benedict elaborates on this theme both in the sections of his *Rule* borrowed from the Master and in chapters more of his own devising. If we can trust Gregory, Benedict knew the terminally destructive effects of murmuring from his own experience of being handed a poisoned chalice. Murmuring weakens and even destroys communities. A desert monk once noted the irony of fasting from meat and wine only to consume the flesh of one another through vicious gossip.[4]

Benedict distinguished between two kinds of murmuring. The first is internal and most destructive of the one who engages in it. Murmuring here is a static in the heart which precludes or at least hampers the ready obedience Benedict expected. The profundity of Benedict's teaching on obedience becomes clear when he insists that exterior behaviour is not enough. If one 'obeys' but complains, whether verbally or in the heart, the obedience is fraudulent (*RB* 5.14–19). Like the Sarabaites who lie by their monastic tonsure, being monks only in appearance, the murmurer's incongruity of intention and action vitiates the superficial obedience.

The second kind of murmuring damages community. Benedict fiercely condemns this all too natural tendency to gripe about the way material goods are distributed (*RB* 34.6–7), the food served at common table (*RB* 40.8) or the quality of the common clothing (*RB* 55.7). The Israelites murmured (Exod. 15:24, 16:2–3), the apostolic community in Jerusalem murmured (Acts 6:1–6), as did the Corinthians (1 Cor. 11:19–22) and every Christian community since. Rarely about theological or spiritual issues, murmuring attaches itself to the practicalities of life. Benedict knew that such complaining, even if low-key and seemingly jestful, can evolve into general dissatisfaction and relentless sniping. Therefore he proclaims an absolute ban on all murmuring (*RB* 34.6, 40.9). He has equally fierce words against interfering with the disciplinary process by defending or championing someone, or by presuming to punish someone without authorization (*RB* 68–9). Lines of communication need to be clear. He knew what happens when those who know only part of a situation fancy themselves to be experts and wade into the fray.

Even so, Benedict shows his pastoral insight by recognizing that sometimes murmuring is understandable and can be forestalled. The superior is to ensure that table servers get a snack so that they can serve without discomfort (*RB* 35.13), to set mealtimes in accordance with need (*RB* 41.5), to ensure that those working in the kitchen get extra help when there are guests (*RB* 53.18) and see to it that clothes fit properly (*RB* 55.8). Obedience is a two-way street. When authority is unreasonable or insensitive, the ideal of ready obedience becomes less and less credible. All of these are Benedict's prescriptions. He replaces the Master's less plausible examples of murmuring with his own more believable ones.[5]

Benedict's insight into the psychology of murmuring helps us to understand what is often described as 'passive-aggressive' behaviour. We know someone who always smiles, conforms to the rules, perhaps even poses as an exemplary monk or nun, while dumbfounding others with occasional flashes of the anger concealed behind the obedient facade. The anger flares out in small but concentrated doses which are often not immediately recognized for the poison they are. The disappointments and resentments that create such poison build up over a lifetime and become harder and harder to salve. By insisting so strongly on the ban against murmuring, Benedict wants his followers to deal with the memories and emotions which make them prone to vicious talk. He also helps to name the resistances we all experience, the calculations and hesitations that accompany every response to a question or assignment.

These behaviours are forms of self-protection, whether

hidden or manifest. The Egyptian monastic writers were keenly aware of the incredibly destructive power of anger. Cassian notes that those who go out into the desert under the guise of perfection are often in fact fleeing the irritating effect of other people. Far from having mastered their anger, they have simply brought it with them into the desert, becoming enraged over trivialities.[6] One monk went into solitude to escape his anger and came to his senses only when he found himself smashing his water jug when it had the temerity to fall over.[7] All of us have done the same sort of thing, and probably been frightened by the sudden outburst of emotional energy. Murmuring comes from those same hidden pools of anger and too easily becomes a way of life. It has destroyed individuals and communities: Benedict's absolute ban was prudent insurance.

Community and Rank

Benedict precisely orders his community in rank from the abbot down to the most junior member. Rank in community determines the order for liturgical tasks and places in choir (*RB* 63.4), and it seems also to have applied to seating in the refectory (*RB* 63.18) and to other assignments.[8] As a matter of simple protocol, of course, rank is useful for dealing with such practical matters. Benedict's optic is less exclusively pragmatic. For him, rank is a vital aspect of mutual obedience and human dignity. In Benedict's monastery, as in the stratified society of his day, everyone had a place. That place, however, was determined not by lineage or social class or accomplishment or job. Those first two markers, perhaps more significant in Benedict's day, and the last two, perhaps more determinative now, are meant to lose their power at the monastery door.

Simply put, Benedict achieves order but abolishes privilege. The major criterion for determining rank is date of arrival at the monastery (*RB* 63.1, 7–8). The secondary criterion is promotion by the superior on the basis of good example and holiness.[9] Age is irrelevant except when it comes to the special needs of children in the cloister (*RB* 63.9, 18–19). Previous station matters not.[10] Even ecclesiastical rank is not to play any role in purely monastic matters (*RB* 60.7, 62.5). Priests and other clerics remain firmly under the authority of the *Rule* and the abbot, who in Benedict's day was not ordained.

The principal distinction in the community was to be that between junior and senior. This was always relative: one's seniors were those who had been at the monastery longer than oneself, and the juniors were those who came after oneself, regardless of their ages. The former, Benedict says, are to be addressed as *nonnus*, a Greek term of uncertain origin which came to mean something along the lines of 'venerable elder'. Its feminine form, *nonna*, is the root of our word 'nun'. Benedict instructs that the juniors are to be called *frater*, 'brother'. Everyone has a title, whether in the eyes of the surrounding culture they merit one or not. Benedict's insistence that no one be called simply by name perhaps reflects his sensitivity to the way that in a status-conscious society addressing someone without a title can be a form of put-down. The clear order he establishes was not meant to oppress the juniors: they are allowed to speak in community meetings because it may be through them that the Lord is speaking (*RB* 3.3). The last in rank is eligible for election as abbot if found to be the most qualified for the office (*RB* 64.2).

Like so many other things in the *Rule*, Benedict's delicate balance tilted dramatically in subsequent centuries. His allowance that clerics could be promoted in rank when exercising liturgical functions later became the basis for dividing male communities into two classes, clerical and lay, with titles proper to each ('Father' and 'Brother'). Among women, social, rather than clerical, forces divided communities into choir nuns and lay sisters. In some cases titles marked these distinctions, as in the English Benedictine custom of calling choir nuns 'Dame' and lay-sisters 'Sister'.

Changes in social conditions and the reforms of Vatican II meant that such distinctions faded. This process occurred more easily in women's communities than in men's. Male communities have typically preserved the Father/Brother distinction of title even as they have restored monastic rank as the fundamental ordering principle in the community. In many male communities the informality of addressing one another simply by name, despite Benedict's ban, has helped to ease the potential of divisive clericalism.

The issue of rank remains significant, and for reasons at the heart of Benedict's concern for it. The countercultural witness of monasticism to the essential dignity of every human person, expressed in Benedict's deliberate rejection of conventional forms of social ordering, remains one of the most important gifts of monasticism to Church and society. Benedictines have not proved themselves to be particularly successful at following their founder's counsel on this vital point. With the collapse of traditional hierarchies in many countries, the danger of false distinction has not lessened but been replaced by new markers of educational and occupational privilege.

The risk is most acute in monasteries which have apostolates requiring specialized training and demanding administrative work. The 'new clericalism' of professional privilege is as insidious as ecclesiastical clericalism or elitism based on social class. The monastic imperative is meant to be far more radical than *noblesse oblige*. Benedict's convictions about mutual obedience are grounded in his teaching that Christian humility really does mean viewing oneself as a sinner. The awareness we can have of our own frailty always exceeds what we can know of another's. Therefore we have no choice but to 'believe with deep feeling of heart' that we are inferior to all (*RB* 7.51) despite our backgrounds, our skills or our education. Even with that recognition of sinfulness, however, Benedict reminds us that we are worthy to be called 'sister' or 'brother,' *nonnus* or *nonna*, for each of us bears Christ to those with whom we live.

OBEDIENCE AND HUMILITY TODAY

All Benedictines would agree that obedience and humility are fundamental aspects of Benedictine life. Perhaps nowhere else, however, does one find so much variety of interpretation and application. Culture and tradition separate not only Benedict's approach from modern ones but modern interpretations from one another. The monastic renewal after Vatican Council II opened up this whole complex of interrelated themes to examination and re-evaluation. Conversation has tended to replace commands, concerns for personal development have emerged, practices which were experienced as cruel or abusive have been eliminated. Communities of women, particularly, are exploring alternative forms of decision-making and discernment, and finding ways to speak about basic monastic values in their own voice.

It would be fair to say that Benedictines are still in a transitional period of learning how obedience and humility can be central monastic values applied maturely and honestly. Reactions against narrow models of obedience or destructive understandings of humility can go and have gone too far in the direction of prizing autonomy above all else. Obedience has typically become a process of discernment, a real gain in terms of mature ownership of a decision but also potentially a means of stalling or resisting an unwelcome invitation. Humility is a difficult concept for those who have suffered from misapplications of it in the past, yet the kind of keen self-awareness that Benedict encourages has never been more necessary than it is now in modern cultures full of fantasies about who and what we ought to be.

This chapter began with the notion of accountability, perhaps the best way to bring together the various aspects of obedience and humility considered here. The Christian life, and monasticism as one expression of it, insists that we are made for life with God and one another rather than for isolation. To know God and others we must understand ourselves, but to know ourselves we must rely on the help of others. The interplay of individual and community is always a matter of learning through experience and negotiation. Benedict uses the traditional monastic terminology of obedience and humility to describe that learning. He orders his monastery in such a way that stumbling-blocks in this process are identified and addressed. Modern Benedictines have begun to work out new ways of doing the same, tugging against countervailing cultural forces that reject the whole project as pointless and perhaps even destructive. Even as we set aside some of Benedict's mechanisms of obedience and humility, we need his insight more than ever.

4. THE SHAPE OF CENOBITIC LIFE

CENOBITES

In his first chapter, Benedict defines 'cenobites' as 'those who live in a monastery serving under a rule and a superior (*abbas*)' (*RB* 1.2). He then devotes the rest of the *Rule* to spelling out what that means. Any kind of community requires roles and structures. However, just because other forms of civic and religious life are communal, follow rules and have leaders, they are not thereby monastic or Benedictine. Benedictine monasteries are shaped by the interplay of three elements: (1) life together in community; (2) following a monastic rule; (3) having a monastic superior who is the spiritual guide for the community as a whole as well as of each member.

'THOSE WHO LIVE IN A MONASTERY': BENEDICTINE STABILITY

A monastery is not an accidental agglomeration of passers-by, but an intentional community of those who have, in their various ways, responded to an inner urging traditionally termed a 'call' or 'vocation'. As one monastic superior has observed, 'we're all volunteers here.' The obedience and humility described in the previous chapter depend entirely upon that basic willingness: daily the decision remains with each person to be faithful or not to the life. Monastic writers have traditionally emphasized the ordinariness and dailyness of monasticism for two reasons: to underscore the continual deliberation needed to remain faithful to a call, and to console

those who have failed with the reminder that tomorrow brings
another chance. The theme goes right back to the Egyptian
desert and its great exemplar, Antony the Great, who made a
new beginning each day.[1] Benedict's Prologue continues to be
read by those who have already responded to its call because
every day is 'today', when the Lord's voice cries out to us (*RB*
Prol. 9–10).

The Benedictine concept of 'stability' is a particular ambi-
ence of obedience. If the false cenobites whom Benedict calls
Sarabaites are deficient by their lack of obedience, the gyrova-
gues or 'rovers' lack stability: 'ever on the move and never
settled [*stabiles*], they are enslaved by their own wills and
gluttonous pleasures' (*RB* 1.11). Cenobites have the benefit of
both accountability and a community in which to live it. In
Benedict's estimation obedience and stability are interde-
pendent. Benedict anchors stability in a community, *in
congregatione*; one is not 'stable' with respect to monastic life
in general (*RB* 4.78). Obedience is within a particular community and over the long haul. Location and duration take
obedience beyond whim or passing fancy. Stability is about
shared history and affections; it is inherently particular. This
means that Benedictine vocational discernment includes
finding the right monastery, not just the right 'order'. Properly
speaking, Benedictines are not an order at all, but a federation
of tribes with a common heritage. The life does not work unless
one feels at home in a particular community.

In his principal chapter on monastic asceticism, entitled 'The
Tools for Good Works', Benedict defines the 'workshop' in which
those tools are used as 'the enclosure of the monastery and
stability in the community' (*RB* 4.78). By emphasizing both
physical location and personal/social connection Benedict
avoids the reduction of monastic life to either element. Neither
cloister nor community alone makes a Benedictine; it is the
energy of seeking God together that bonds place to people in
this unique way.

Although Benedict hoped that monasteries would be largely
self-contained (*RB* 66.6–7), he allowed his monks to leave the

monastery on business (*RB* 50–1, 67) and foresaw that there might be reasons for joining another monastery (*RB* 61.5–11). The *Rule of the Master* ends with a description of the shut gate of the monastery (*RM* 95.22–14), but Benedict closes his *Rule* by urging his readers to hasten to their heavenly homeland (*RB* 73.8–9). Gregory tells us that Benedict's monks evangelized their neighbours at Monte Cassino; most of Europe was converted to Christianity by monastic missionaries.

For monastic women there was always a stricter understanding of cloister, especially since the sixth-century *Rule for Virgins* by Caesarius, Bishop of Arles.[2] There was by no means a single view about enclosure for women among the male monastic legislators. Donatus of Besançon wrote a *Rule for Virgins* in the seventh century based in part on Caesarius' but setting aside the rules of strict enclosure. Although total enclosure was sometimes practised, especially in France, until the end of the thirteenth century it was rare in England and Germany.[3] Abbess Hildegard of Bingen (1098–1179), for example, preached and taught throughout Germany and France. The stricter view was mandated by Pope Boniface VIII in 1298, who by the first word of his decree, *Periculoso*, revealed the mindset of the times: 'danger'. Despite the Pope's wishes, observance of enclosure varied greatly and it was by no means universally accepted. New initiatives of the Council of Trent in the 1570s gradually achieved more universal and strict compliance, with the grills, turns, and extern sisters necessary to make it all work. A spirituality and theology of enclosure developed along with the practice. Some communities even made it an additional vow. In time, enclosure came to be regarded by many communities as a privileged insurance of their contemplative character.

Nineteenth-century missionary Benedictinism in North America discovered, after heroic attempts, that to maintain a traditional form of enclosure for monastic women was simply impossible on the frontier. Benedictine nuns found themselves with responsibilities toward local people similar to those of their brother monks, who had never been encumbered by such a strict interpretation of cloister. The women paid canonical penalties for changing their practice of enclosure, losing the traditional monastic 'solemn' vows made by their European sisters and being canonically redesignated as 'sisters' (*sorores*) rather than 'nuns' (*moniales*), a distinction still used (unfairly and often pejoratively) to distinguish members of some congregations of Benedictine women from those who live a more enclosed form of monastic life.[4]

The application of the Benedictine notion of 'stability in community' varies greatly among different Benedictine traditions. There remain some disagreements among Benedictines about how far the notion can be stretched before breaking or becoming indistinguishable from the organizational structure of other religious orders.

The narrowest definition would be found among the strictly enclosed communities which engage in no external apostolates and typically do not assign members away from the monastery. An intermediate variety would be those which allow members to live away from the home monastery for pastoral or educational purposes. Stability 'in' the community for them does not have a geographical imperative, though one is a member of and returns to a particular community. This model would apply to most North American Benedictine men and women and to many European communities of Benedictine men.

Finally, there are Benedictines who vow stability to a congregation rather than to a particular community and can be assigned (and reassigned) to any monastery of the congregation. The origins of this tradition are in the reform movements of the fourteenth century exemplified by the Italian Abbey of Santa Giustina, which established highly centralized congregations similar in many respects to more recent orders like the Dominicans. Olivetan Benedictines retain a strong congregational structure, as do the contemplative Sisters of Perpetual Adoration in the United States and the many missionary congregations of Benedictine women such as the Australian Sisters of the Good Samaritan, Tu tzing or the

English Benedictine Sisters of Our Lady of Grace and Compassion.

The spiritual value of stability lies in commitment. Like everything else in monastic life, stability works best when it is wholehearted, without escape hatches or preserves of autonomy. Having committed both spiritual and material fate to a particular community, a Benedictine has a stake in keeping the community focused on what they are meant to be about. She must be faithful to the Work of God, *lectio divina*, personal prayer. She has committed herself to being present to her sisters in the monastery. She works in support of their life together. She attends chapters and community meetings, welcomes guests and newcomers to the community. She helps to care for those who are ill or in distress, and helps to bury the dead. She works at seeing Christ in the people with whom she lives. Where better to find him?

Benedict's 'Tools for Good Works' (*RB* 4) include several maxims about dealing with other people, both inside and outside of the community. The whole chapter makes a fine examination of conscience and is used as such in many communities. Benedict adapts his maxims from those in the *Rule of the Master*, introducing new elements which highlight charity toward other people.[5] Running throughout the chapter is concern for honest and authentic relations with others. He begins with a reprise of the commandments but then zeroes in on anger, deceitfulness, apathy, malice, jealousy and all the other forms of self-protection and aggression that fragment community life. Among the dozens of counsels are these: 'Your way of acting should be different from the world's way. Do not hold on to deceit in your heart. Never give a false peace. Do not abandon charity. Do not aspire to be called holy before you really are. Love chastity, hate no one, shun jealousy, do not act enviously, do not love conflict, flee arrogance.'

Such practical bits of advice surprise readers who expect a more 'constitutional' tone to the *Rule*. They remind us, however, that monastic community is built upon the same foundation as any Christian community, the practice of the commandments. At the end of the Prologue Benedict even defines monastic life as running on the *via mandatorum Dei*, 'the path of God's commandments' (*RB* Prol. 49). He reminds us in the 'Tools for Good Works' that we do not run alone.

Because Benedict places stability at the centre of his monastic programme, we must also grapple with the shadow side of stability, which consists of complacency and the monastic affliction known as *accidie*. Monastic routine can dull alacrity, and each day can become much like another, without any sense of electric response to God's call. Dull patches are inevitable in anyone's life. The discernment is to detect when the patch has become the whole, when one has settled into a spiritual hibernation for which there never seems to be spring. The Prologue of the *Rule* calls one out of such torpor and to take to the path of God's commandments. Stability is about keeping on the path, not about chaining oneself to the starting post. Monastic complacency can have an aggressively defensive side to it, a menacing smugness that is perhaps the least attractive form of monastic existence.

The other danger is the antsy listlessness called *accidie*. Identified by Egyptian monks as a particular danger to hermits, cenobites know it also. A day becomes something to be got through, its demands seemingly endless and equally unappetizing. Anything promising diversion has great appeal, but genuine satisfaction lies always out of reach, with someone else, in doing something else. Evagrius Ponticus, the acute fourth-century monastic psychologist, described it this way: 'it seems that the sun hardly moves and that the day is fifty hours long; the monk constantly looks out the window, walks around outside, peers at the sun to figure out how long until dinner time; there arises a dislike for the place, for the monastic life, for work; the monk thinks that love has fled from among the brothers and that there is no one to provide any encouragement.'[6] *Accidie* depends on the con that life used to be – or will someday be, or could somewhere else be – better than it is here and now. Not so much melancholy as restlessness, *accidie* urges its victims to surf the World Wide Web of life in search of illusory fulfilment.

The risk in *accidie* is that one either abandons monastic life entirely or does so internally by escaping into fantasy as a protection from the demands of commitment and community. Anyone who has been married or has made a similar commitment to a person or a group knows the temptation. Early monastic writers urged hard work as a particularly apt remedy for *accidie*, joining work, of course, to a battery of reality therapies designed to counteract the allure of fantasy and self-deception. Work was not an escape from painful experiences but one aspect of healthy living. Work at that time was simple and manual, with clear and immediate results. The prescription of work as a cure for *accidie* is somewhat trickier today, when work is often neither simple nor immediately productive. Work can become an escape from *accidie* rather than a cure. Benedict prescribes service of one another, mutual obedience, work, spiritual guidance and annual renewal in Lent as ways to keep monastic life grounded in the freshness of each moment.

SERVING UNDER A RULE: THE COMMON LIFE

The idea of a monastic 'rule' seems self-evident to us after centuries of Benedictine conditioning. Monastic history, however, shows that the very concept of an objective norm applied to all members of a community was neither obvious nor uncontroversial. The anchorites of the Egyptian desert taught by example and tailored ascetical practices to the needs of individuals. They defined themselves over against cenobitic fondness for rules, as in this story about Abba Poemen:

> A brother asked Abba Poemen, 'Some brothers live with me; do you want me to be in charge of them?' The old man said to him, 'No, just work first and foremost, and if they want to live like you, they will see to it themselves.' The brother said to him, 'But it is they themselves, Father,

who want me to be in charge of them.' The old man said to him, 'No, be their example, not their legislator.'[7]

Despite this attitude, the Egyptian monk Pachomius, who is considered the founder of the cenobitic life, learned the necessity of a common rule through painful experience. Like Benedict, his first try at presiding over a community was disastrous. His mistake lay in trusting that a community could function solely on the basis of the superior's humble modelling of service, as in the relationship between elder and disciple described above by Poemen. The fragmentary accounts of that episode are painful to read, though fascinating in their preservation of the founder's learning curve.[8] After praying over his experience of living with monks who refused to follow his example and abused his generosity, Pachomius realized that a community needs clear expectations and he provided them. His monasteries were highly organized communities with an evolving set of policies.[9] In this way they were like the communities for which Basil the Great provided in his so-called *Long Rules* and *Short Rules*, which were cast in the form of replies to questions about monastic policy.

The evolution from the concept of 'rules' to the particular kind of spiritual and legislative document known as a 'Rule' occurred in the Latin world.[10] At the end of the fourth century Augustine wrote a cogent, structured guide for his monastery in Hippo; this document, known as the Praeceptum, or 'Instruction', is the first text we would recognize as a 'Rule' in Benedict's sense.[11] Augustine's *Praeceptum* and the Latin rules written for the monks of Lérins,[12] an island off the southern coast of France, are the direct precursors of the *Rule of the Master* and The *Rule of Benedict*. These rules covered basic topics thought to be essential to cenobitic life: spiritual authority and leadership; the monastic horarium; common and personal prayer; admission to the community; discipline and punishment.

The fluid nature of early rules is evident in the successive revisions of those from Lérins and in Benedict's radical reworking of the *Rule of the Master*. Benedict allows that his own work is provisional; though he foresaw that his *Rule* could be used by other communities (*RB* 55.1–2), he also admitted the possibility of revising its liturgical details (*RB* 18.22). We know that the common western practice in the centuries immediately after Benedict was to base monastic life upon a variety of rules, drawing upon the best aspects of each. Benedict's *Rule* was merged with the *Rule of Columban* to create a 'mixed rule' (*regula mixta*) followed in monasteries of the Irish mission to the Continent; in Spain, the *Rule of Benedict* was combined with rules by Isidore and Leander.[13] Only slowly, in part owing to the Carolingian campaign for monastic order spearheaded by Benedict of Aniane early in the ninth century, did Benedict's *Rule* become regarded as an exclusive, stand-alone, monastic rule.[14]

There were gains and losses in such uniformity. Fixing a three-hundred-year-old text as a norm for monastic life opened a gap between *Rule* and practice that has only widened since. The *Rule* immediately required supplementing by local 'customaries', books of policy and interpretation which modified and amplified its prescriptions. The later emergence of groups of monasteries linked to a common founding or reforming community led to the development of 'constitutions' which legislated in areas the *Rule* did not and also mitigated or revised its teachings. Sometimes constitutions were accompanied by 'declarations' interpreting each chapter of the *Rule* according to the needs of that particular group of monasteries.

With the *Rule* incapable of revision or amendment since its canonization in the ninth century, the practical prescriptions contained in it quickly declined in usefulness while its spiritual teaching and presentation of the basic cenobitic framework endured. Even these were adapted to address emerging needs. Therefore we learn more about monastic life over the centuries by reading customaries and constitutions than by reading (the surprisingly few) treatises or commentaries on the *Rule* itself. It is not surprising that an appeal to literal observance of the

Rule has characterized reform movements from the time of Benedict of Aniane in the ninth century to the Cistercians in the twelfth, the Trappists in the seventeenth, and various 'primitive observance' movements more recently.

We do not know exactly when the *Rule of Benedict* was first used by women. In the Latin world there had already been rules prepared specifically for monastic women. Augustine's *Praeceptum* was adapted for female use quite early,[15] and Caesarius had written a rule for women shortly before Benedict's time (the *Rule for Virgins*). The early use of the *Rule of Benedict* by women's communities was, as in men's communities, as part of a 'mixed rule.'[16] The Carolingian reform began the process of establishing Benedict's *Rule* as normative and exclusive for women and men alike. There is no extant early rule written by women for women, though medieval feminized and adapted versions of the *Rule of Benedict* survive in both Latin and vernacular languages.[17]

The use of this originally male monastic rule by women has often raised more than linguistic questions. In the twelfth century the Abbess Heloise complained to her mentor Abelard that the *Rule* was manifestly unsuited to women.[18] What she initially presents as the inability of female weakness to meet the *Rule's* heavy demands soon turns into a critique of its normativity. Since not even men can follow the *Rule* exactly, she observes, what is the point of imposing it as a norm for anyone? More fundamentally, why insist on practices that in themselves are unimportant? Is not the gospel enough? She asks Abelard to provide her nuns with a rule that is specific to women and their needs. This Abelard does, though without setting aside the *Rule of Benedict*: he interprets, modifies, and supplements just as everyone else has since Benedict laid down his pen.

Whether used by women or men, the *Rule* needs always to be read and lived in the present, within a particular culture and in a particular set of circumstances. Any appeal to the authority of the *Rule* is inevitably partial, for strictly literal interpretation is a chimera. By the ninth century liturgical developments had already made the *Rule* somewhat out of date, and the questions Abbess Heloise raised about gender and practicalities of daily life remain at issue today.

Artificial lighting, computers, audiovisual technology, new economic realities and social attitudes are incontestable and indeed often welcome facts of life. Therefore the interpretative standard has to be authenticity to Benedict's spiritual wisdom rather than a fundamentalist approach to the letter of the *Rule*. The renaissance in monastic studies in the last hundred years has brought a much keener awareness of the theological and literary background of his work. By understanding Benedict's sources and his *Rule* better, we have gained a keener sense of his own interpretative attitude toward the earlier tradition and a greater possibility of working with that spirit for the sake of monastic life today. That spirit can help us to bridge the gap between letter and practice.

THE MONASTIC SUPERIOR

The central figure in Benedict's monastery is the one who bears the title 'abbot'. The word, of Aramaic origin, means 'father'. Used by Egyptian monks, it passed into Latin from Greek and endures in modern languages. The feminine form 'abbess' is used in some monasteries of women, though male and female communities can also be led by someone called a 'prior' or 'prioress', actually the more ancient Latin designation for the superior of a cenobitic community.[19] By Benedict's time, however, the titles of *abbas* and *abbatissa* had become standard. Everything Benedict says about the abbot of his male community has been applied by the tradition equally to abbesses and prioresses. For the sake of clarity and inclusiveness I will generally refer to the monastic 'superior' when applying Benedict's teaching about the abbot to Benedictine life through the centuries.

Benedict expects the superior to be the quintessential monastic Christian. The superior is not set apart from the rest of the community, but is a strong sign of Christ's presence in their midst. The *Rule* might seem to suggest that the superior is the pinnacle of the organizational pyramid, the one from whom all lines of authority radiate downward. Indeed, the language Benedict uses – '[the superior] is believed to represent Christ in the monastery' (*RB* 2.2), 'the abbot, because we believe he represents Christ, is called lord and abbot' (*RB* 63.13) – is impressive. It would be a mistake, however, despite the superior's tremendous authority, to view the role in terms of power or status: the superior 'is to be for them, not over them' (*RB* 64.8).

There is nothing in the *Rule* to suggest any prestige or privilege accruing to this office. Utterly and entirely a position of service, the role goes badly wrong when seen in any other way, whether by superior or by community members. Like everyone else, the superior is accountable to the *Rule*[20] and, more particularly, to Christ, whose deputy she or he is.[21] Benedict expects that the superior will be somehow chosen by the members of the community themselves (*RB* 64.1), just as bishops were at that time. In accord with the custom of the times, the office would have been held for life. Benedict underscores the daunting burden of divine accountability in his reminders that the superior is responsible for the members of the community in the same way a shepherd is accountable for the sheep of a flock.[22] The office has meaning only in relationship with those who have come to serve under a rule and a superior. Benedict's shepherd imagery may seem quaint to some readers, but because of its biblical resonances he employs it with great conviction.

As he did for obedience, Benedict describes the superior's role twice, at either end of the *Rule* (*RB* 2 and 64). Both descriptions emphasize the love and discernment the superior must always use when relating to those in the community. Benedict borrows a maxim from Augustine (as he was prone to do), reminding the superior 'to strive to be loved more than feared' (*RB* 64.15). The primary task, Benedict insists, is to love everyone in the community.[23] The love is to be inclusive and even-handed (*RB* 2.16–22), but none the less specific and deliberate. It involves teaching, personal concern and reproof. Thus the superior must try to understand each person in order to find a way to love even the apparently unlovable, and to love each one in the way that person requires. Hildemar, the early commentator on the *Rule* and himself an abbot, modelled the love between superior and community on that of Christ and the disciples: the superior must love those in the community in order to teach them, and the members of the community must love the superior if they are to obey. It is the love between them that makes everything possible.[24]

The superior has three main tasks: to teach, to arrange and to command (*docere aut constituere vel jubere*, RB 2.4). First and always the superior is a spiritual guide and teacher. This commission is grounded in the search for God.[25] Everything depends on the superior's own fidelity to *lectio divina*: the superior must be, as Benedict prescribes, 'learned in divine law' (*RB* 64.9) and able to draw on the 'medicine of Holy Scripture' for the benefit of the community (*RB* 28.3). Commands and teaching must be recognizably based in the 'divine law', i.e., the Bible (*RB* 2.5). Benedict requires the superior to be a skilled teacher, able to employ a variety of strategies in both instruction and pastoral care.[26] The key virtue is *discretio*, a word which means both 'discernment' and 'moderation'.[27] Comparing the superior to someone removing rust from a pot, Benedict reminds us that scraping the pot too hard will break it (*RB* 64.12). Recognizing that overly zealous correction of others can be a form of projection as well as an act of aggression, he tells the superior to be always mindful of her or his own weakness (*fragilitas*) lest the bruised reed be crushed (*RB* 64.13, citing Isa. 42:3).

The superior's administration of the monastery must foster the search for God by preserving peace.[28] Benedict charges the superior to ensure that grievances about food, work, clothes, rank do not interfere with the primary purpose of the life.[29] The superior is to be especially solicitous of the sick, the excommunicated and guests.[30] The superior ensures that the community is called to the Work of God at the proper time,

approves Lenten resolutions and assigns work.[31] As steward
over the material goods of the monastery, the superior ensures
that all things are distributed according to individual need.[32]
In such tasks there are helpers, such as deans, a cellarer, and
if necessary, an assistant superior whom Benedict calls the
praepositus (prior).[33] Benedict expects the superior to take
counsel from the whole community or, for lesser matters, from
senior advisors (*RB* 3).

Benedict is also wary of diluting the superior's authority. He
allows for delegation of both practical and spiritual matters
but fears alternative power centres within the community.
Unlike the author of the *Rule of the Master*, however, Benedict
is not paranoid in his protection of authority; indeed, he notes
that the superior must not be restless, anxious, prone to
extremes, stubborn, jealous or oversuspicious. Such people, he
concludes, 'are never at peace' (*RB* 64.16). None the less, his
reminders that all things are to be done at the superior's
bidding or with permission, and his hesitations about the office
of *praepositus*, the 'number two' figure in a monastery, seem
to have an air of insecurity about them. His real concern,
however, was more likely to have been to protect the relationship between superior and community from anything that
would erode its strength or lessen mutual accountability. In
this he shows forethought rather than paranoid anxiety.

Benedict legislates that the superior be chosen by the community, but leaves the manner of selection vague. Either the
whole community or a group within it of 'sounder judgement'
makes the selection. They are to be free in choosing whomever
they see fit even if it be the most junior member of the monastery. Over the centuries Benedictines have employed different
forms of discernment and selection of superiors. Election of
some kind has been the norm but in the Middle Ages was not
always actually practised or genuinely free. Already in the
Carolingian period, abbots and abbesses were often appointed
by king or bishop rather than elected by the community.[34]
The privilege of exemption from such external interference, as
Cluny had, still did not mean that superiors were actually

elected by the community; the great early abbots of Cluny appointed their successors. In the early thirteenth century the Fourth Lateran Council finally required election of both abbots and abbesses.

Abbots and abbesses of larger monastic houses were typically drawn from the nobility. They could too easily lose their pastoral role, living according to their social rather than monastic standard and directing their energies increasingly toward political affairs or management of estates. Other monastic officials had to pick up the slack. For this reason, Abelard insisted that an abbess not be from the nobility unless absolutely necessary. If she were, he feared, she would confuse her family obligations with her conventual ones to the detriment of the community.[35]

In wealthy monasteries in the late Middle Ages the abbatial office was often completely separated from the actual life of the monastery and became a gift of patronage used to reward loyal service to the crown or, as often the case with women's communities, a way to keep wealth within a particular family. A share of the monastery's revenues went with the title; such an 'abbot' or 'abbess' no longer had to be resident at the monastery or even in vows. The practice had begun as a way to give the community a powerful external protector, to whom was 'commended' the office of superior, but became inevitably dominated by political and financial concerns. This practice, of course, obviously bore no relation to Benedict's conception of the relationship between superior and community.

The Reformation, monastic reform movements, the French Revolution and its continental aftermaths eventually allowed for new beginnings in the European monastic families. The earliest kinds of reform, such as those of Monte Oliveto in the fourteenth and Santa Giustina in the fifteenth centuries, featured short-term (but real) abbots elected or appointed for each house, though a considerable amount of governing authority remained at the congregational level. Their prohibition of lifetime superiors ensured that the office was not viewed as a sinecure or power base. Although this was progress

over the commendatory approach, the short terms of office
(three or four years, without possibility of succession) inevitably emphasized the administrative aspects of the office
rather than the long-term pastoral relationship Benedict
envisaged. The Council of Trent as part of its reform of the
religious life insisted on election of all superiors by secret
ballot.

The renewal and refounding of monastic life in the nineteenth century typically restored the traditional model of a
lifetime superior, elected by the members of each monastery.[36]
Since Vatican II there has been a growing tendency toward
terms, whether indefinite (i.e., until the superior determines
it is time to make way for someone else) or fixed. The ideal of
lifetime tenure presumed by Benedict has come to be seen as
a burden both to superiors and to their communities. The office
has always been difficult, though it is perhaps more so in an
increasingly complex world and in a challenging period in the
life of the Church generally and religious life in particular.

The changing understanding of obedience in western monasteries since Vatican II has meant that superiors and
community members talk more, disagree more, and generally
have to devote more time to discernment than was the case
when major changes of assignment could be made with a note
on the bulletin board. Traditional forms of deference to
authority, derived from court or prelatial circles, have been
abandoned. Many communities of women, for example, have
set aside the custom of addressing the superior as 'Mother' in
order to encourage more mature ways of relating. Growing
awareness of deep-seated illnesses such as chemical and sexual
addictions requires sensitivity to psychological issues and the
dedication of ever more time to pastoral care. And, of course,
communities still expect their superiors to be teachers of the
Rule and able to reflect upon its implications for their lives.

Benedict cautions superiors not to show more concern for
material and temporal matters than for the health of the souls
committed to them (*RB* 2.33). None the less, the demands of
external relations, financial pressures, fundraising, manage-

ment of apostolates, and legal concerns of every kind have increased tremendously in the last fifty years. Too easily a superior and community members can conveniently distance themselves from one another by viewing the office primarily as administrative. Managers are less threatening than are spiritual authorities. Shuffling assignments is easier than addressing serious personal problems. To deal with a superior only about jobs or community business is to avoid a potential source of challenge to a life which may have become complacent or laced with *accidie*. It is also to forego a significant opportunity for guidance and support. It is true that superiors cannot be all things to all people, despite Benedict's urging. Real engagement with someone else's struggles is not always possible and does not always work. But if the very essence of the office is a relationship of love, that relationship runs far deeper and should be evident in much more than juridical and administrative tasks.

'To teach, to arrange, to command': but all in accord with the Law of the Lord (*RB* 2.4). Benedict's comprehensive understanding of Christian leadership defies reduction to a list of tasks. He ends up emphasizing the qualities of the officeholder rather than the duties of the office. Spiritual leadership depends on spiritual authority, which finally is not about office or title but about the recognizable presence of the Holy Spirit in one's life. The monastic superior must be open to the Spirit and the members of the community open to seeing the Spirit at work in their midst through their superior. It is a sublime conception, possible only on the basis of faith.

5. THE DISCIPLINED LIFE

'KEEP DEATH DAILY BEFORE YOUR EYES'

One of the phrases thought to capture the essence of Benedict's spirituality is 'Keep death daily before your eyes' (*RB* 4.47). Benedict is not recommending macabre obsession with the inevitability of physical decay. Rather, he knew that awareness of mortality exerts a unique power to focus the mind and heart on essentials. Death is the definitive encounter with God, who meanwhile keeps a watchful eye on all that we do. Benedict asks us to consider how we wish to go to God, and reminds us that now is the only time we can be sure of for making ourselves ready. Throughout the Prologue runs that urgency of *now* coupled with God's invitation to get to it.

From the outset of this study we have seen how awareness of God's presence pervades the *Rule*. Every practice and discipline of the monastery should heighten awareness: this is the meaning of self-renunciation, the lessening of me for the increasing of God. Benedict's predecessors in the monastic life knew and taught that such lessening took time and proceeded through stages. The exterior renunciations of family, status and possessions were a beginning, and continued to create regret and anxiety. But the real battle with self is always in the heart. A person can surrender bank accounts, car keys, houses and credit cards, but the heart and its many possessions come with us wherever we go.

The external and physical disciplines of the monastic life establish parameters and space for the transformation of mind and heart that Benedict calls *conversatio morum*. The phrase is tautologous, meaning something like 'manner of life and ways of acting'. Some have emphasized the idea of repentance, reading *conversatio* as if it were *conversio*, but the sounder interpretation is that by *conversatio morum* Benedict simply means the monastic way of life. It includes the obligations to prayer and *lectio* we have already described; fidelity to *Rule* and superior as fundamental aspects of cenobitic monasticism; and, more basically, living out the commandments as a monastic Christian. Just like any other serious pursuit, monastic life has its own skills and training regimens. In this chapter we turn to the various disciplines of the monastic way. These practices have been traditionally described under the heading of 'asceticism', a severe-sounding word that means simply 'training'.

PHYSICAL ASCETICISMS

The *Rule of Benedict* is not a markedly severe document. When judged by the social and monastic standards of its day, it allowed Benedict's monks adequate sleep, decent nourishment, sufficient material goods and a manageable round of liturgical and individual prayer. Over the centuries these prescriptions have been adapted or abandoned as standards of living (and monastic wealth) have risen. There have been and remain monastic and religious orders with far more rigorous regimens. Some reform movements within the Benedictine world have focused on recapturing earlier rigour or introducing new severity, as was the case of the Cistercians in the twelfth century and the Trappists in the seventeenth.

Benedict's monks had about six hours of sleep in the summer (supplemented by an hour's siesta) and nine hours in the winter.[1] Their rhythm of resting and rising varied according to season because artificial light was costly and inefficient. Anyway, rural life runs according to the sun. Their sleep was uninterrupted: i.e., breaking sleep in the middle of the night for a liturgical office and then returning to bed was not an asceticism to which Benedict subscribed. Once his monks were

awake, they stayed awake. Nor does he perpetuate the ancient
practice of all-night vigils for Sunday and feast days, as does
the Master.

Benedict legislates for two cooked dishes at the main meal
of the day, plus fruit or fresh vegetables if they are available.
Each person received a substantial loaf of bread and a ration
of wine, doubtless drunk diluted with water as was customary.
Fish and fowl were eaten; red meat ('the flesh of four-footed
animals') was not.[2] During about half the year (Easter to
September) there were two meals a day. Otherwise the meal
was in mid-afternoon (September to Lent) or, during Lent,
even later (*RB* 41).

These prescriptions pertain to the main meals of the day.
Early monastic custom was to have a single meal in mid-
afternoon ('the ninth hour' of a day reckoned from sunrise).
Modern western readers accustomed to three feedings a day
need to remember that Benedict's pattern remains the norm
in many parts of the world and, indeed, is increasingly common
among weight-conscious or frantically busy westerners. When
Benedict's monks ate, they ate sufficiently, and when the work
was particularly hard, they were fed more (*RB* 39.6 and 40.5).
Benedict shows his own bias toward abstemiousness in his
remarks about gluttony (*RB* 39.7–9, 40.5) and his grudging
concession of wine (*RB* 40.6–7) but seems resigned to the fact
that varieties of temperament and physiology make it impossible to legislate alimentary asceticism on a uniform basis.

Of other physical disciplines Benedict says little. He was
sceptical of baths, but allowed them as often as useful for the
sick and occasionally for others (*RB* 36.8).[3] His monks had
their own beds – a luxury in that day – with adequate bedding,
and they all slept in the same large room (*RB* 55.15). They
had a change of clothes, sandals and shoes. A nicer tunic and
cowl were issued for travel (*RB* 55.1–14). Each had a knife,
and writing or sewing utensils as needed (*RB* 55.19; cf. 22.5).
Basic items were to be made available 'to remove any excuse
of need' (*RB* 55.19). The approach was eminently sensible.
There are no bizarre ascetical practices. Self-flagellation or

standing in ice-cold water or wearing hair shirts are not part of his conception of the life. The basics, lived faithfully, are more than enough.

Succeeding centuries brought predictable changes in physical disciplines. The advent of clocks allowed the horarium to be standardized. The tendency over time has been to retire and to rise later, often for reasons dictated by the work of a particular community: farming monasteries get up earlier than those whose primary work is educational. The amount of sleep probably has changed little. The typical modern Benedictine gets much less sleep in winter than Benedict's monks did, and perhaps a little more in summer.

Since Benedict's time the monastic diet has tended to become better and more ample. Meal times and frequency tend to mirror those of the surrounding culture. Meat has been permitted in some monastic congregations for centuries and is now typically found in non-Cistercian houses. Increasing concern for hygiene has, of course, made bathing an expectation rather than a concession. The common dormitory was preserved in many congregations and communities until fairly recent times, though modern needs for privacy and the fact that many people today have never shared a room before coming to the monastery have made private rooms the norm.

The declining role of physical asceticisms in modern monastic life has been balanced to some extent by heightened attention to psychological issues and the disciplines necessary for emotional maturity. Work has also grown in significance to become the great asceticism for many Benedictines. Benedict's goal was balance, giving the body what it needed to be healthy and to serve well without allowing bodily comforts to exercise tyranny. This is easier when and where luxury is impossible. Today it is difficult to distinguish between necessity, constructive allowances and excess. That task of discernment has to come home to each individual.

RENUNCIATION OF POSSESSIONS

Early monastic men and women were sometimes simply called 'renouncers' (*apotaktikoi*). What people noticed about them was what they had 'given up', the breaks they had made from conventional behaviour. Benedict makes a somewhat different, and more specifically cenobitic, point. Cenobites make an exchange. They exchange their own clothes for those of the monastery, their own possessions for those distributed by the community, their own wishes for the expectations of common life and the commands of the abbot and other superiors. Benedictines generally do not make specific vows of poverty and chastity,[4] though they do profess obedience. Poverty, chastity and every other practice and virtue thought to be essential to living the commandments as a monastic Christian are understood within the vow of *conversatio morum* and also as aspects of monastic obedience and stability.

We have already seen the centrality of obedience and stability to Benedictine life. Their practical corollary is physical dependence on the monastery for one's material needs. Benedict steps out of his moderate persona when he takes up this topic, as he does for murmuring. He is fanatical on the issue of private ownership. His issue was not that his monks had things, for that is unavoidable. The problem is amassing possessions outside the network of interdependence that lies at the heart of cenobitic community. If those who have given control of their bodies and wills[5] over to the community retain an area of self-management beyond the access of others, they have compromised the fundamental monastic commitment.

John Cassian brilliantly describes the problem by caricaturing an acute case of obsession with money. Writing for a monastic audience, Cassian defines the vice of avarice in terms of desire for financial independence. Such a desire dissolves the bonds between individual and community, and finally dissolves the community itself. Cassian writes:

This vice [of avarice] begins by suggesting to the monk

some excellent reasons why he should retain some money for himself. He complains that what is provided in the monastery is not sufficient, even for someone strong, and that he must have something of his own in case he becomes ill . . . He thinks he cannot bear to remain in the same place, in the same community, and needs some money to escape.

Having conceived the desire for money, he then manages to get some:

Having money to provide for his wanderings, and ready at any time to take off, he answers impertinently to all commands, and complains about whatever he sees. Even though he has a secret supply of money, he still complains that he doesn't have enough shoes or clothes, and is indignant that his needs are not being met more speedily. He is not content to turn his hand to any work, but finds fault with every task the community requires to be done . . . The result is that he can never remain content in the monastery, living under the discipline of a rule.[6]

Benedict hopes to forestall the whole sick cycle by ensuring that the members of his community have what they need (*RB* 55.18–19). The important principle is accountability, not destitution. Benedict links accountability to the superior, who either directly or through the cellarer distributes every necessary item.[7] Distribution is governed by relative need rather than absolute equality. The point is both pastoral and ascetical: pastoral in that an individual's unique situation and needs are the basis for decision, ascetical in that one has to surrender validation of those needs to a person or a process beyond oneself.

Some of the other great early monastic writers were acutely sensitive to the different needs of different kinds of people. Augustine, for example, recognized that those from poor backgrounds would have a different understanding of need than those who had formerly been wealthy. He was worried lest the latter be proud about their former status or dramatize the extent of their renunciation. Equally problematic was the possibility that those from poor backgrounds would see the monastery as a place to acquire what had formerly been denied them.[8] A story was told about the famous desert father Arsenius, who scandalized some by using a pillow when he was ill. The tut-tutters were silenced when it was pointed out to them that Arsenius, having been a Roman of senatorial rank, a resident of the imperial palace and tutor of the Emperor's sons, had made a far greater renunciation of material comforts than had his critics, many of whom were now living better as monks than they had as poor shepherds.[9]

Determining need is a matter of discernment rather than of absolute rules. Does 'need' mean bare necessity, or what is needed for me to grow and to flourish? Today we would incline more toward the latter approach than was done in earlier times. For us to discern genuine need, and to avoid misuse of things or of people, we have to learn how to confront our desires, which are many and often quite subtle, and then to surrender those which prevent us from loving God and neighbour. Desire in itself is good: it makes us get up and set about the search for God, fuelling the ascetical work of learning how to love. But we have an incredible knack for desiring the wrong things, or getting hung up in little desires while the great ones go unsatisfied. Confronting all of our desires, small and great, sick and healthy, is the only way to know what our needs truly are. Only then can our cravings become the basis of compassion toward ourselves and others.

WORK

Benedict's monks worked several hours a day. Unlike the Master, Benedict permitted field work and foresaw periods of particularly intense labour,[10] though he does not mandate a particular kind of work required of everyone (other than, of course, routine tasks such as serving at table). He viewed work as both productive and preventative: the chapter on 'The Daily

Manual Labour' opens with the maxim, 'idleness is the enemy of the soul' (*RB* 48.1).

Benedict does not present work in terms of self-fulfilment or creativity. For him, necessity, discipline and service were the primary values.[11] Benedict follows monastic tradition, which saw hard work as the best remedy for *accidie*. Physical activity is good for the body, as is a salutary fatigue. But the early monastic teachers also knew that work of any kind, if done conscientiously and deliberately, takes us out of ourselves. A task finished or at least well-begun marks a day as fruitfully spent, banishing the dread of empty vastness which underlies *accidie*.

Benedictines have proven remarkably adaptive to a variety of kinds of work, even within the same community. Benedict recognizes individual talents by allowing for the exercise of skilled crafts, though his primary concern in that chapter is guarding against the danger of self-importance based upon work (*RB* 57). Many know that medieval monasteries developed scriptoria; the copying of manuscripts had long been a classic monastic work. Necessary for internal purposes and lucrative as a business enterprise, copying was physically and psychologically more demanding than one would think. Manuscripts also provided opportunities for monastic artists in the painted pages and illuminations prepared for Gospel and other notable books. Earlier we noted the beginnings of Benedictine educational work, which has since become the mainstay of many communities though strongly resisted by others.

The healthiest communities contain a variety of skills and an appreciation for all of them. Each kind of work has its own benefits. Ideally everyone would have both manual and intellectual work as part of their daily assignment. This has become less feasible with the increasing professional demands placed even upon Benedictines in communities without schools. Specialization can bring with it the risk of thinking oneself indispensable to the community or above the common expectations of attendance at choir or table. This is precisely the danger Benedict was alert to in his chapter on 'The Artisans of the Monastery' (*RB* 57). It requires a good deal of self-knowledge and maturity to do a job well without having one's identity and self-worth entirely bound up with it.

In many Benedictine communities, even those considered particularly 'contemplative' in orientation, work has become the major monastic asceticism, consuming more and more time and attention. Traditional asceticisms, of course, are understood as such and oriented toward a goal. Often intellectually enervating, modern monastic work can sometimes leave little energy for prayer and *lectio divina*. Work, despite its ascetical qualities, is often not regarded as a fruitful discipline pointing beyond itself to a spiritual goal, but becomes an end in itself whether for financial or personal reasons. The result can be a crushing burden of tasks which are never finished and a constant (if unacknowledged) guilt about neglect of monastic duties. Time becomes feverishly coveted. Modern monastic avarice is often more about time than about money, and Cassian's portrait of the avaricious monk can be transposed to describe someone obsessed with schedules and the protection of 'my' time.

If the reality of modern monastic life is the greater prominence of work, then the theology and spirituality of work require renewed attention. Benedict's fairly narrow view of work will not be enough for us. We can highlight the elements of service and the salutary obedience in performing necessary tasks, but will also need to articulate a positive view of individual creativity as well as a spirituality which can deal with failure when jobs do not work out. The effect of failure can be devastating if a community's culture has no way of understanding the inevitability of mismatches or appointments that are less than ideal. Awkward avoidance of the topic or advising people to 'offer it up', however spiritually fruitful that might be for some people, cannot be the limits of pastoral care to those who have troubles in their work. Equally we must delight in tasks well done, whether our own or those of others. If humility is nothing more than honesty, then congratulation is obligatory.

CHASTITY

In the classic lists of monastic vices, lust and avarice sit side-by-side (along with gluttony) as disorders of human desire. Having surrendered the pursuit of sexual gratification and the potential misuse of other people for that purpose, Benedict expects monastic Christians to relate to one another freely and respectfully. He says little directly about chastity,[12] and never mentions friendship. However, the superior is to love the members of the community and to be worthy of their love in return.[13] Benedict sees tenderness toward the elderly and children as perfectly natural (*RB* 37.1), and urges his community to love those junior to them in rank (*RB* 4.71, 63.10). These references to relationships within the monastery, as well as Benedict's teaching on meeting Christ in the other and on mutual obedience, help us to understand his views on monastic chastity.

The *Rule* presumes that everyone receives love and obedience as well as gives them. Gregory's *Dialogues* present Benedict as a man capable of attracting both friends and disciples. Whatever the accuracy of the stories, their portrait of a loving Benedict has been treasured by monastic tradition. Benedict's predecessor John Cassian wrote a conference on friendship (*Conf.* 16), and some seven hundred years after Benedict the Cistercian monk and Abbot of Rievaulx in Yorkshire, Aelred, wrote two major treatises on the theology of monastic friendship.[14] Benedict leaves us no such theology, but by concluding the *Rule* emphasizing 'pure brotherly or sisterly love' he leaves us with the assurance that monastic Christians are to support one another in the common journey to God (*RB* 72.8). Indeed, at the beginning of the *Rule* he notes that hermits are prepared for their solitude by the 'support of many' in the cenobium (*RB* 1.4). An eighth-century *ordo* from Benedict's monastery at Monte Cassino continues this tradition:

Among them let there be such love that if someone has to

be away for a long while on community business, until he returns all should miss him with a love so great that no mother could miss her only son more. When he returns to his own, let them fall upon his neck with a kiss, fulfilling with fraternal affection what the Lord said in the Gospel, 'Then you will truly be my disciples, if you love one another' (John 13:35).[15]

The ascetical aspect of chastity lies in its convergence with humility. Both virtues are finally about self-awareness and transparency before God and others. John Cassian describes the perfectly chaste person in this way:

> The same at night as in the day, the same in bed as at prayer, the same alone as when surrounded by a crowd of people; seeing nothing in the self in private that would be embarrassing for others to see, nor wanting anything that the omnipresent Eye [of God] detects, to be concealed from human sight. (*Conference* 12.8.5)

Such transparency meets others on the ground of their need rather than on one's own turf. The surrender of control over others in mutual obedience and chaste love parallels closely what Benedict teaches about material goods. All aspects of God's creation, all things given from God's hand, are received as a sacred trust.

The issue of interpersonal relationships has become more prominent in monastic life in the last few decades. The severe line toward 'particular friendships' typical of pre-Vatican II monastic formation sometimes created an unhealthy atmosphere of suspicion and repression of feelings for others. Now there is greater recognition that because people come to monasteries to seek God in community, they need help in learning how to forge strong, durable and honest friendships both inside and outside the community. Those who enter monasteries today often have a strong sense of their own sexual identity and some experience of intimate relationships. Naturally they seek to integrate these aspects of themselves into their monastic lives. Not all of their experiences will have been happy. Painful memories or fears of intimacy have to be faced and dealt with. But the joys of human love come to the monastery as well, and must always be a cause for thanksgiving even as one learns how to love in monastic chastity. Like every other aspect of monastic life, chaste loving is largely a matter of discernment.

RELATIONSHIPS OF SPIRITUAL DISCERNMENT

Benedict was heir to the monastic practice of offering thoughts to a spiritual elder for help in discernment. The relationship underlying this practice was the entire basis of Egyptian desert monasticism. The interactions between these *abbas/ ammas* and their disciples are depicted for us in the thousands of sayings of the elders passed on by early monastic scribes.[16] The principle behind the practice was that we cannot have a clear view into our own hearts. Spiritual vision is clouded by unresolved and often conflicting desires which are murkiest when our own lives are in question. Thoughts, questions, obsessions need to be brought out into light and air where they can be seen for what they are.

The point seems obvious but the practice is difficult. The internal resistances of denial and shame collude with in-hibitions generated by embarrassment and the need for approval by others to keep vitally important issues cycling endlessly in the heart. Only with the patient companionship of another human being can one find the courage to speak aloud what has been preoccupying the mind and heart. It is the speaking itself that brings peace. The elder's words are simply commentary on the real work done by the one who has opened the heart.

In early cenobitic life the relationship between monastic superior and community members contained many elements of the elder/disciple model, including the practice of bringing thoughts forward for discernment. Soon the emphasis came to be placed more on the confession of sinful thoughts than on the offering of all thoughts, a shift explainable by pressures of time and numbers of people seeking counsel. Both the practice of manifesting thoughts and the increasing emphasis on sinful thoughts are evident in the *Rule of Benedict*.[17] Benedict depicts the abbot of his monastery as pre-eminently, though not exclusively, the spiritual mentor to the community. Others could share in this role of spiritual discernment and authority.

Benedict refers three times to the practice of confessing thoughts. Among the 'Tools for Good Works' he advises, 'When evil thoughts come into your heart immediately dash them against Christ and disclose them to a spiritual elder' (*RB* 4.50). The fifth step of humility is that one 'not hesitate to make a humble confession to the superior of all evil thoughts coming into the heart or evil things done in secret' (*RB* 7.44). Finally, sins which are not of a public nature are to be revealed to the abbot or to one of the spiritual elders (*RB* 46.5).

In the first and the third cases, Benedict has broadened the ministry of spiritual guidance beyond the superior alone. This was a deliberate departure from the *Rule of the Master*, which jealously protects the abbot's authority and uses the deans as conduits to the abbot rather than as spiritual elders in their own right.[18] Benedict's terminology of the 'spiritual elder' reflects a return to earlier practice and language.[19] The pastoral pre-eminence of the superior is in no way lessened, as Benedict's two chapters on the abbot's care for the excommunicated and the obstinate make clear (*RB* 27–8), but he recognized that those in positions of authority are not always best placed to deal with a particular person or situation (*RB* 27.2–3). Bernard of Monte Cassino tries to resolve the tension between 'abbot' (*RB* 7.44) and 'abbot or spiritual elders' (*RB* 46.5) by arguing that because the confession of thoughts requires more counsel than authority it need not be made to the abbot, while the confession of sins requires both and is properly reserved to the abbot.[20]

We have already explored Benedict's approach to public excommunication and reconciliation. Here the issues are private. Despite Benedict's emphasis on sinful thoughts or deeds, surely the context was one of discernment and desire for understanding. The values he praises are openness and humility, not thought control. In these relationships of spiritual guidance, whether with superior or with spiritual elder, community members could identify the barriers to stability, *conversatio morum* and obedience. They could seek help in resolving conflicts with other people. They could begin to understand the dynamics of their emotional and spiritual lives.

The actual content of the discussion between individual and spiritual elder or superior would have depended on the particular situation. The important point here is that Benedict saw not just the value but the necessity of such a practice. He knew the taxonomy of eight major faults brought from Egypt to the west by Cassian. This invaluable diagnostic tool would have assisted the work of identifying and addressing individual difficulties.[21] The original list of gluttony, lust, avarice, anger, sadness, *accidie*, vainglory and pride was later adapted by Gregory the Great into a catalogue sometimes known as the seven capital or deadly sins. Numerous medieval monastic treatises about the moral life were based on this inventory.

Benedict was not describing sacramental confession as it was understood and practised in later Christian traditions of east and west. In his day sacramental penance was still confined to major, public sins and was more a matter of ecclesiastical discipline than individual counsel. The 'confessors' in Benedict's monastery were not priests, and abbesses heard their nuns' confessions just as their male colleagues did.[22] The practice he describes would play a role in the development of private penance, but the monastic origin of Benedict's recommendation keeps it firmly in the realm of discernment rather than canonical regularity. It was more akin to what we would call spiritual direction. Benedict reminds us that following the rules, even the *Rule*, is not enough. Genuine commitment to monastic *conversatio* means the kind of accountability possible only when one human being opens the heart to another and experiences forgiving acceptance. Integral to the monastic programme as Benedict presents it, the practice of manifestation of thoughts, sinful or otherwise, strikes at that self-will and self-sufficiency of which he was so wary.

Benedict's approach is still evident in the eighth and ninth-century customaries and commentaries which view 'confession' in terms of spiritual clarity rather than ecclesiastical 'penance'. One of these notes, 'better that we accuse the devil than be ourselves at fault. For if we always confess his evil insinuations, so much the less will he be able to harm us.'[23] Hildemar remarks that thoughts cannot be discerned by just anybody: thus Benedict's reference to a 'spiritual' elder.[24] At this early stage, both a common confession of faults[25] and confession of individual faults within a communal setting (the so-called 'chapter of faults') were the customary means for the avowal of public failures prescribed by Benedict.[26]

As private sacramental confession became established in the western Church it became a part of Benedictine life. There was some effort to relate Benedict's prescriptions to the medieval penitential system. A late tenth-century English customary has the abbot or his delegate hearing confessions on Sundays, and alludes both to the fifth step of humility and to the private avowal of faults described in *RB* 46 to justify the practice.[27] Medieval customaries for male communities included a time for confession in the daily schedule (usually between Lauds and Prime) and delineated qualifications for the monk-priests who served as confessors. At Eynsham in the thirteenth century, confessors are expected to be friendly as well as faithful. Those who come for confession must be able to love and to trust their confessors in order to reveal willingly the secrets of their hearts. The confessors are reminded not to give burdensome penances since 'the entire life of a religious, even if it lasted a thousand years, would still be penitential.' A single psalm would suffice under ordinary circumstances.[28]

The rise of sacramental confession, which was made an annual obligation for all members of the western Church by the Fourth Lateran Council in 1215, complicated Benedict's understanding of the charismatic role of spiritual guidance.

For several hundred years already abbots had been ordained as priests, muddying the distinction between their charismatic and hierarchical roles. Abbesses heard confessions from their nuns, but could not grant sacramental absolution. A chaplain provided by a nearby monastery of men or another priest was needed to pronounce the sacramental formula required by canon and custom. The result in both men's and women's communities was that sacramental confession often became the dominant mode of formal spiritual guidance, though naturally counsel of various kinds was always part of monastic formation and experience.

Since Vatican II the practice of frequent sacramental confession has declined among Benedictines as it has in the Church at large. For some, relationships of spiritual direction (which may or may not include confession and sacramental absolution) have become the place for discernment and counsel. Monastic women have renewed their own practice of spiritual mentoring and often done a better job than their brothers in making the opportunity available to those beyond their monasteries. Many Benedictines have found psychological counselling enormously beneficial, while others need the support of twelve-step or similar groups in order to remain honest with themselves and others. They need an explicitly Christian and monastic complement to these practices, though sometimes psychological help is easier to find than good spiritual guidance. For others there is a vacuum, the danger both the desert tradition and Benedict warn against. Benedict challenges us to be honest at the most intimate level of our lives. Whatever form that honesty takes, it is non-negotiable.

6. TIMES AND SEASONS OF BENEDICTINE LIFE

MONASTIC TIME

The variegated nature of monastic time energizes Benedictine stability. Prayer, meals, work occur at specific hours. Bells ring to mark not only the hours of the clock but the times of prayer as well. When Benedictines meet, they soon start comparing schedules, for the horarium of a community tells much about its life and character. There are also longer-term rhythms in every monastery, particularly the seasons and feasts of the liturgical calendar and the celebrations unique to the community. Profession days, patronal feasts, significant anniversaries, jubilees, retreat weeks and days of recollection mark time in ways distinctive to Benedictine life. Deaths sanctify time according to their own, inscrutable, schedule. Visitors to monasteries always note these rhythms, finding in them a coherence of religious intention and practice that seems more elusive elsewhere.

Benedict created a complex set of reckonings of time for his monastery. He varied the times for prayer, meals and work from weekday to Sunday, fast day to feast. In the *Rule* he calculates time according to the ancient method of twelve day hours and twelve night hours keyed to the sun. In summer, for example, the entire period of daylight was divided into twelve 'hours', making a summer daytime hour considerably longer than one of our standard hours. The twelve summer night-time hours were then much shorter than the daytime ones. The proportions were reversed in the winter and in balance at the equinoxes of spring and autumn. The monastic horarium changed seasonally to take maximum advantage of daylight and to suit the spiritual demands of each liturgical season. In summer days were long and full, and nights all too short. During winter, days were relatively short but there was much more time for sleeping.

In the *Rule* the major liturgical seasons of Lent and Easter controlled everything. Easter was the fulcrum of the entire year. On Easter all schedules changed, whether for prayer, meals, or work. Lent meant more time for *lectio divina*, Easter meant more frequent meals. Spring and summer (Easter to October 1) brought more work.[1] The system was complex, but it kept everyone attuned to both natural and liturgical rhythms. Light and darkness, sowing and harvest, penance and resurrection shaped the experience of prayer and attention to bodily needs.

Since Benedict's day timekeeping has been perhaps the only aspect of monastic life that has become simpler. Clocks have made fixed, equal hours the chronometric standard. The availability of relatively inexpensive artificial lighting mitigated the urgency of Benedict's requirement that as much as possible be done by light of day (*RB* 41.8). Benedictine schedules today rarely feature a substantial variation between winter and summer except where work requires it, whether that be field work or school calendars. Sleep patterns remain constant, prayer schedules more or less the same throughout the year, allowing some variation for Sundays and feasts. The liturgical rhythm has become less a matter of schedule than of customs and symbols linked to the major seasons of Advent and Christmas, Lent and Easter, and other major feasts and occasions.

None the less, the basic principle of sanctifying and marking time remains vital to monastic life. The light in church is different in April than it is in January. The return of sweets at Easter is duly noted. Profession days re-energize commitment and funerals provide the *memento mori*, the reminder of death, that Benedict considered to be so important. Monastic life needs salt to keep its vigour and savour, and the calendar provides the salt.

The annual cycle of seasons and feasts is the background for each individual's cycle through the stages of monastic life. The monastic path contains markers of call, entry, initial formation, monastic profession. For those who entered the monastery young, there comes a long haul toward the final years; for everyone there is the passage through death to new life. Each stage has its imperatives and challenges.

CALL AND ENTRY

The Prologue of the *Rule* is its invitation to monastic life. Speaking through texts taken largely from Psalms 15 and 34, Benedict notes how God invites us to awake from the sleep of unconcern and to get moving on the path toward fullness of life. There is little specifically monastic about the call until the Prologue's very end. The phrase 'school of the Lord's service' finally proposes the location and mode of the Christian obedience proper to cenobitic monasticism (*RB* Prol. 45–8). The invitation is open to all who 'long for life and desire to see good days' (*RB* Prol. 15, quoting Ps. 34:12).

Benedict says nothing about the age, social class or education of those who hear the call. The invitation is universal, and therefore the paths to monastic life are innumerable. Benedict provides for the special cases of infants offered to the monastery by either noble or poor families (*RB* 59), clerics who wish to enter the monastery (*RB* 60), and those transferring from one monastery to another (*RB* 61). He notes that a novice may be illiterate (*RB* 58.20). That array of possible scenarios begins to suggest the vast territory covered by monastic aspirants. The key point is always discernment of a call to cenobitic life in a particular community. Other factors bear on the discernment but are not at its core.

Today Benedict's ample conception of the monastic vocation is more evident than it has been for many centuries. Candidates for monastic life, at least in western countries, tend to be older than was the case before Vatican II, when many entered monasteries in their late teens. These older candidates often bring an abundance of professional and personal experience to their communities, and the monasteries are not always good at accepting and incorporating this background into the common life. In Asia and Africa monasteries often draw mostly young candidates who need education and will mature into adulthood in the monastery. The growth in these communities may far outstrip that in Europe or the Americas, where communities experienced the same kind of exuberant expansion during earlier phases of their history. The challenge of diversity is stark in places like Africa or India where newcomers from various tribes or cultural groups must find a way to live together, often pushing against outside social pressures that would keep them apart.

The *Rule* is not a programme of monastic formation or a chronological map of the monastic life, and Benedict places his discussion of monastic admissions late in the text. Only in Chapter 58 do we read the laconic criteria for entry: 'the concern must be whether [the newcomer] truly seeks God and is serious about the Work of God, obedience and challenges. All of the hardships and difficulties by which one goes to God are to be explained' (*RB* 58.7–8). It is here that Benedict describes monastic life as 'seeking God',[2] a phrase aptly chosen by many as a motto for Benedictine life.

Following established custom, Benedict advised testing the newcomer's fervour by refusing immediate entry into the monastery. There is to be an initial probation of a few days during which even the guest quarters are closed to the potential recruit. Admission to the guesthouse then follows as an additional probationary period before entry into the novitiate.[3] The Benedictine novitiate is both a place and a process. As place, Benedict describes the novitiate as the location where the novices study, eat and sleep under the direction of a skilled senior monk (*RB* 58.5–6). As process, it means deepening the novice's familiarity with both *Rule* and community. Benedict requires a full year's probation, marked by formal readings of the *Rule* and reconfirmations by the novice of intention to persevere. After twelve months, that intention becomes final and public in the act of monastic profession before the entire community.

Benedict's profession rite powerfully communicates a definitive change of life. What was pious intention becomes concretized in deliberate action. Having given away all possessions and renounced all external claims, the novice makes the Benedictine promises of stability, *conversatio morum* and obedience. Written up as pledge and contract, the vows are placed on the altar in an act of covenant. Manifesting dependence on the community by prostrating before them and asking for their prayers, the newly-professed is 'from that day counted as one of the community' (*RB* 58.23).

Benedict's concept of renunciation could not be stronger. Joining the community through profession means giving away everything one had before entering, either to the poor or to the monastery, 'without keeping any of it for oneself, knowing well that from that day forward one no longer has authority over even one's own body' (*RB* 58.24–5; cf. 33.4). Benedict has the new member change clothes in the oratory immediately after the promises and prayers. The point is to lay aside what was one's own and to put on the things of the monastery. The emphasis falls not on the 'monastic' appearance of the new garb, though monastic men and women already wore distinctive clothing in Benedict's day, but on the exchange of personal, private property for communal property. Everything one will have from now on will come from the monastery.

Given their centrality to monastic identity it is little surprise that the rites and practice of monastic formation and profession have undergone complex development since Benedict's time. The time-frame has varied considerably. The Rule's one-year probationary period was often shortened in the Middle Ages. Cluny, for example, reduced it to a month or even less.[4] Later reforms restored the full year, and more recent introduction of a three-year period of temporary vows before final profession has further lengthened the probationary period.[5]

Modern practice also includes a trial period before the novitiate, extending Benedict's 'four or five days' to several months or even a year. Some congregations require a two-year novitiate, and Roman Catholic canon law allows the period of temporary profession to extend up to nine years, though three or four years is typical. In male Roman Catholic communities, candidates for the diaconate or priesthood also have a course of studies followed by ordination. Although since Vatican II there has been progress in disentangling monastic formation from preparation for priesthood, the distinction between them is not always as clear as it should be.

Like other aspects of monastic liturgy, entry and profession rites became more and more elaborate in the Middle Ages.[6] The clothing in monastic garb, or at least in some of it, gradually migrated to the beginning of the novitiate. For men, the tonsure, a distinctive haircut which signified the clerical or monastic state, accompanied the conferral of the habit.[7] For women, there was a ceremonial betrothal to Christ, sometimes symbolized by wearing a wedding dress which was then exchanged during the ceremony for the habit and veil of a novice. This also involved a haircut, a dramatic gesture in days when women outside of religious life never wore short hair. At profession, the hood or a different veil and the full choir robe worn over the habit were conferred.[8]

Monastic profession attracted both baptismal and nuptial symbolism. To symbolize death to an old way of life, the newly-professed were covered with a funeral pall as they lay prostrate in prayer. Rings were blessed and given to monastic women. A prayer of consecration was added to the actual profession of vows to confer a special blessing, like the nuptial blessing at weddings or consecratory prayers at ordinations. For women, the ancient rite of 'consecration of virgins' was either joined to the profession rite or celebrated at a later time, associating these two distinct forms of religious dedication.[9] The most recent reforms of profession rites have replaced the former view of monastic profession as a 'second baptism' with a re-commitment to baptismal life. Typically much of the bridal imagery has been discarded for women, although the ring has been retained as a sign of permanent commitment.

Most communities that use a monastic habit have modified Benedict's understanding of monastic clothing. They typically confer the habit, or much of it, at the beginning of the novitiate, long before any formal renunciation of property. Benedict's close linkage of disappropriation/profession/clothing is thus broken, and the sequence becomes instead clothing–first profession–disappropriation/final profession. The habit thus symbolizes the monastic lifestyle rather than disappropriation and final commitment to a particular community. Final profession then requires the conferral of additional garments or symbols.

In communities where the habit is worn exclusively, it is a genuine expression of monastic simplicity. The traditional Benedictine habit, however, is not suited to all occasions. It functions well as a formal garment for choir, meals and other occasions but other clothes are usually worn for manual labour or exercise. Monasteries which have modified the habit or replaced it with a multi-purpose garment worn at all times come closest to Benedict's way of thinking, which was that of the early monastic tradition.

When it came to the actual vows professed by Benedictines, the introduction of lay brothers and lay sisters in the Middle Ages opened a canonical distinction between 'solemn vows' and 'simple perpetual vows'. The former required total renunciation of any ownership of property and entailed a special prayer of consecration, while the latter forbade the use and administration of property, but not ownership itself. In monastic life the distinction between kinds of vows was more than canonically significant. Those in simple perpetual vows, the lay brothers or sisters, were not allowed chapter rights and thus could not elect the superior nor vote on major community matters. Those privileges were reserved to choir monks and nuns in solemn vows. In monasteries of men, the choir monks were all ordained to the priesthood.

When Benedictine nuns arrived on the American frontier

they found that some aspects of their European monastic life (such as strict enclosure) were not possible. They were thenceforward denied solemn vows and also lost the full Latin Benedictine Divine Office.[10] Unfortunately the canonically second-class status decreed by ecclesiastical authority led to misplaced judgements about the monastic character of American Benedictine women. Among the men, the distinction between choir monks in solemn vows and lay brothers in perpetual vows lasted until the 1960s, and was often the source of resentment and arrogance about who were the 'real monks'. The reforms of Vatican II and the more recent revision of Roman Catholic canon law have left the various congregations free to determine the obligations of final profession for their members while requiring equal application of both obligations and rights. Progress toward recovering Benedict's understanding of monastic profession has been real.

'PERSEVERING IN THE MONASTERY UNTIL DEATH'

'From that day the novice is to be counted as one of the community' (*RB* 58.23). When the process of initial formation ends, a Benedictine still has to keep moving along the path of the commandments. With less supervision, perhaps less emotional zeal and with decreasing energy, reliance on inner spiritual resources and maturity becomes essential. The years following profession confront monastic Christians with the normal stages of human development as young adulthood shades into middle and then old age. Each transition tests the promises of stability, *conversatio morum* and obedience.

Cenobites have the advantage, increasingly rare in western cultures, of living in a household with people ranging in age from their twenties to their nineties (and sometimes even beyond). Benedict was aware of the special needs of both young and old, and extended the 'authority of the Rule' to protect them from overly-strict interpretation of monastic dietary norms (*RB* 37). We have already seen his understanding of how the relatively junior and senior should relate to one another (*RB* 63.10–12, 15–16). The young can gain from the old a sense of where the monastic life should (or should not) take them. Those in the middle can see in the young their own beginnings in the monastery, and in the old they are reminded of their inevitable destination. The old live daily with death, just as Benedict prescribed (*RB* 4.47), seeing members of their families and peer group die one by one, being tested daily in their Christian faith that the best is, indeed, yet to come.

Most Benedictine experience seasons in the monastic life, and the years immediately after final profession bring their own challenges. Work often becomes an increasingly important part of one's life. Modern Benedictines, perhaps especially in North America and western Europe, can fall into measuring self-worth by their job. Benedict's warning to the artisans of the monastery not to overestimate their contribution to the community (*RB* 57.2) becomes increasingly relevant today as even cloistered communities often support themselves through high-tech enterprises. The one who knows how to operate the computers, like the other 'experts' in the monastery, be they administrative, scholarly or agricultural, is not absolved of humility.

Meanwhile the perils of *accidie* are ever near as decades of prayer and work stretch ahead with no significant personal landmarks in sight. Issues submerged during the formation process may reappear, new questions arise, relationships sour or collapse. All of these are perfectly normal parts of adult life that occur in monasteries as well as in families. The way through them is always by the asceticism of discernment. It can be tempting to think that one is 'done' with formation at final profession and no longer needs spiritual guidance. As noted in the last chapter, the monastic tradition consistently warns against the illusion of self-reliance. Even after decades of monastic life the presence of another person to listen and to help one to understand is essential. The manner and intensity of spiritual guidance may change over time but somehow it has to be there.

For those in the prime of life, at the height of their talent and productivity, keeping death daily before one's eyes or being mindful of the last judgement are not reflexive attitudes. They require cultivation. Prayer and *lectio* become most important for the long haul during the very time of life when they are most likely to be overshadowed by the other demands of community. When immersed in work, it is easy to discount the inner labour of preparation for the day when work will no longer be central or even possible. To devote all attention to the verbs in the sentence of a life is to neglect its subject and object. Everything that Benedict says about the monastic life is designed to prevent such short-sightedness.

Benedictines hear the whispers of mortality like everyone else. Awareness of death becomes less and less optional. The reconciliation of enduring desires with narrowing possibilities is an exercise of profound asceticism. Benedict provides little guidance for the middle decades of life, a lacuna which may reflect the short life span of former times as much as anything else. In Benedict's day someone who survived until age twenty could typically expect to die before fifty, and would experience the symptoms of old age before then. The shortcomings of Benedict's theology of work are perhaps equally explicable by that reality of comparatively brief lives. One of the challenges to monasticism in more recent times has been sustaining people through a greatly expanded middle part of the journey, normally twice as long as what Benedict might have foreseen as typical. Alternative futures become not only imaginable but attainable as social pressure to remain faithful to a monastic commitment has dramatically relaxed. Benedictines leave their monasteries just as spouses leave their marriages, and for a similar mix of reasons. Benedict's path of the commandments begins to feel like laps on a track. Each turn brings its own challenges and each lap requires another 'yes'.

Benedict says only a few words about the old. They evoke compassion and deserve the practical concession of eating early (*RB* 37.2–3). His many references to 'seniors' are not meant to be taken in purely chronological terms but within the ranked order of the monastery, though the 'spiritual elders' (*seniores spiritales*) were surely validated by substantial experience of the monastic life (*RB* 4.50, 46.5). Again we find ourselves in a different world. Benedict's era when ten per cent of twenty-year-olds could expect to see seventy is a far cry from modern monasteries full of active septua- and octogenarians. Old age can now be almost as long as early Christian adulthood, and monastic communities have not always been adept at finding meaningful and appropriate work for their older members. It is sad indeed when the elderly Benedictine's best companion is the radio or television.

HEAVEN

Benedict had a keen sense of the inevitability of death and a firm belief in heaven. He expected his followers to come to the monastery in hope of heaven. The reward he envisaged for them lay beyond the sweetnesses of this life, in the 'heavenly homeland' to which we are meant to be hastening.[11] He tells us nothing of his own conception of heaven, unlike the Master who concludes his chapter on humility with a colourful description of paradise.[12] But Benedict also allows more room for joy in the present life than does the Master,[13] though we remain none the less on pilgrimage toward another, and better, place.

Such otherworldly orientation is rare among modern Christians. We neglect Benedict's perspective at our peril. The Christian life always runs along a narrow ridge between angelism on the one side and hedonism on the other. We are made to be immersed in the natural order, though we need training to contemplate its beauty more deeply and truly. Benedictine monasteries are often located in places of natural beauty, consist of handsome buildings, are decorated simply but beautifully in a way that prizes artistic expression. In the Middle Ages the monasteries and their churches were often oases of beauty, whether in the opulence of Cluny or the starkness of the Cistercian churches with their clear glass and simplest of lines. The challenge has always been to remember that even the sublimest art, whether visual, literary, or musical, may be a sacrament of divine beauty but can never be an end in itself.

Benedictines have comfortably accepted the optimistic anthropology of the early Church which recognized that we are naturally desirous of the beautiful, but our desires must be challenged and clarified. On the emotional and sexual level the training comes through chastity; the intellect is re-formed through *lectio* and study; the senses are taught to hear and to see deeply and truly through encounter with the arts. We know the eternal most through its traces in the world, whether in the faces of those we love or in the work of gifted hands. Faith reminds us not to mistake the ephemeral for the enduring. The binocular vision of now and forever, the Zen of the moment and the 'assurance of things hoped for' (Heb. 11:1) lies at the heart of the monastic enterprise. Each monastic day is a lifetime in miniature, just as each lifetime can be seen as dawn and dusk, with strength rising to its zenith and dwindling toward nightfall. Benedict believed time had been redeemed, and that it led somewhere. Though the path of the commandments leads inevitably to death, there is a door in the wall, a door which opens into the heavenly homeland for which Benedict so longed.

CONCLUSION:
MONASTICISM FOR THE WORLD

Benedictines have always been deeply involved with the Church and world in which they live. Monasteries have traditionally welcomed guests and pilgrims, and many people who will never live in a monastery have found the *Rule* to be the 'surest of guides' for their lives as Christians. Most Benedictine monasteries have oblate programmes that invite people to affiliate themselves with the community and to profess fidelity to the *Rule* as their situation in life allows. There continue to be experiments with more intense forms of affiliation such as lay communities or live-in programmes lasting weeks or months at a time. Some speak of 'temporary vocations' like the Buddhist practice in those cultures where spending time in a monastery is a normal part of growing up. People see in the Benedictine way of life what they want for their own: a structure of prayer and work that is bigger than individual efforts. Books on the spirituality of Benedictine life, usually written by non-monastic Christians, continue to multiply as writers want to share their own discovery of Benedict and his teaching with those who may never have considered monasticism to be even faintly relevant to their own situation. For those who have discovered Benedictine spirituality its theory may be appealing, but the real draw are the practices: *lectio divina*, the Divine Office, hospitality, and so on.

Benedictines are gratified and amazed by this surge of interest. They are also humbled by the good zeal of oblates and friends that often seems to outstrip their own. However superficially different from the vowed monastic life the situations of these people may be, many of them are deeply rooted in both practices and attitudes learned from the *Rule*. What they may see more clearly than those in the monasteries is that Benedict does not pretend to teach other than the fundamentals of the Christian life. People who believe in God's gift of life in Jesus Christ come together to 'devote themselves to the apostle's teaching and community, to the breaking of bread and the prayers' (Acts 2:42). That community of belief, prayer and service ranges in size from hermits to hundreds. It crosses ecclesial lines, for Benedictine spirituality is a legacy to the whole western Church and a point of union with the eastern Christian traditions which draw from the same wells Benedict did. The ecumenical significance of biblically based common prayer is immense. The Benedictine cloister's spiritual embrace extends far beyond its visible walls, usually much farther than those who live inside ever realize. It seems fitting, then, to conclude this study of Benedictine spirituality with an eye toward its application beyond the vowed monastic life.

Because Benedictine life in so many ways is nothing special, it can be hard to pin down what makes it so distinctive. It *is* distinctive, perhaps more by the combination of elements than by the elements themselves. This book has tried to show both the elements and the way Benedict and his followers have built from them a distinct way of life. Sometimes 'Benedictine values' such as hospitality and community are abstracted and made so generic that they become a kind of spiritual etiquette attractive to all, offensive to none, and meaning little in concrete terms. For Benedict, however, teaching and example, theory and practice, are inseparable. To isolate particular themes from the experiential context of the Christian common life, whether lived in a monastery or not, is to miss the genius of the *Rule*.

In thinking of Benedictine monasticism as a message for all Christians, we need to start with the *Rule*. It is the common ground of everyone and everything in the monastery, for all alike, from superior to novice, regard the *Rule* as the norm for community life. This obvious point is often seen best by Benedictine oblates, who live without the complex customs, structures and policies which govern monastic communities. When the *Rule* is one's only cloister, its spirit can be breathed directly.

Because no one follows the *Rule* exactly, everyone has to engage with it directly in order to work out how it applies to their life. That work of interpretation and application may be communal, as in monasteries, or individual, as it is for those who use the *Rule* in secular life. However and wherever it is done, reading and learning the *Rule* are essential. When Benedictines read the *Rule*, they read it as they read the Bible, looking for its basic theology and spirituality, interpreting and discerning its instructions for practice. The language of the *Rule* and the insights which underlie even its most evidently obsolete provisions shape Benedictine life.

Benedict's most fundamental insight in the *Rule* is that we seek God through ordinary means. God is already here, in and among us, if only we can learn to see Christ and hear his voice in those with whom we live. Gregory the Great's stories about Benedict in the *Dialogues* contain hints of his mystical experiences but the *Rule* presents just the basics of monastic life. Benedict would have us structure each day with several exercises of attentiveness to Christ, each a form of listening and responding to God in prayer. The development of these exercises over the centuries and the various arrangements of them within the Benedictine tradition past and present suggest that the key to mindfulness lies not in precision of detail but in the ensemble of practices. Individuals have the same freedom as communities to find a mix that works for them. For it to be 'Benedictine', it would contain both liturgical and personal prayer, be grounded in *lectio divina*, and heighten awareness of how we stand before God as both sinful and saved.

The *how* of standing before God is what Benedict tries to evoke in his teaching on obedience and humility. These relational virtues, even though they are ultimately about our relationship with God, cannot be learned in isolation from other people. Benedict's sensitivity to social relations within the monastery comes not so much from a desire to preserve harmony as from a hope that every interaction serve growth in obedience and humility. Like so many early monastic teachers, Benedict had learned that left to ourselves we can too easily develop a false confidence about our progress in the spiritual life. Other people remind us by their examples, good and bad, and by our interactions with them, fortunate and unfortunate, of how far we have yet to go. Life with others gives us that clearer sense of ourselves that comes by seeing through their eyes, as well as the means by which we turn that humbled self into a vessel ready to be filled by the love of God. The learning that Benedict describes as obedience and humility occurs through loving regard for others, just as Christ's own identity as Son of God among us stands forth most brilliantly from the Cross. Every family and workplace can be a 'school of the Lord's service' where actions and attitudes are interpreted and directed according to the model of Christ. It is, as always, a matter of how – and what – one sees.

The formal structures of cenobitic life would seem to be its most distinctive and non-exportable aspects. Vowed life in community, commitment to the *Rule* and to obedience, create the matrix of accountability that sustains the whole monastic enterprise. But Benedictines are not alone in making vows of dedication and commitment. Long-term undertakings come in many forms and have similar challenges. Acknowledging the spiritual authority of a spouse makes marriages as well as monasteries work: remember Benedict's teaching on mutual obedience. The same lessons of openness and trust can be learned in committed partnership as in monastic profession. Neither comes with any guarantee of success, though both have great potential.

Although some would argue that the present-day culture of western countries is uncongenial to self-sacrifice, others observe that modern western countries are the most ascetical societies in human history. For one thing, it takes determination and hard work to survive within market-driven economic systems. The ugliness of many modern cities and the brutal social inequalities denying too many people basic human dignities are involuntary asceticisms. Meanwhile, millions of over-fed people diet and exercise to attain an ideal figure. The difference between these asceticisms and the monastic ones is enormous. The latter are both freely chosen and directed toward spiritual goals. Each of Benedict's disciplines, whether physical, spiritual or intellectual, served growth toward God and other people.

For many the opportunities afforded by monastic life would be unthinkable luxuries, and its disciplines would be far less onerous than their own. The only possible justification for monastic life and its spiritually oriented asceticisms is a conviction that the goal Benedict proposes is essential to human wholeness for monastic and non-monastic people alike. Today most Benedictines have considerably modified their founder's ascetical prescriptions. They run the risk of losing sight of the larger significance of their daily life and practices. The *Rule* reminds everyone that even the most mundane aspects of our lives can cultivate love. Benedict encourages all of his readers to ask what larger purpose directs their daily lives and then to reshape practice to accord with goal.

Benedictine monasteries apportion specified time to prayer, work, meals and recreation. Weaving in and out of this daily routine are the seasons and feasts that enliven the ordinary. Every human being lives a scheduled life, though few mark the turning points of the day, the week, the year as deliberately and explicitly as Benedictines do. Although the milestones of education, commitment, and family life have their own rituals, the integration of these major events into the spiritual journey is not always evident. Benedict teaches us that the rhythms of both communal and individual life need to be recognized and respected.

The natural rhythms of work and rest, prayer and conversation, are basic to human fulfilment. Worry about time and its use easily preoccupies modern people who feel that they have less and less of it. If prayer becomes optional, competing with all of the other options of daily life, it tends to lose out. It needs protected space each day. Benedict ensures that protection by making the schedule of prayer fundamental, with everything else keyed to that basic rhythm. It is an obvious move, but deeply subversive of attempts to put other things first. It is also easier in practice for cenobites than for those living outside of monastic community. But how well do any of us really live by the principle of 'prefer nothing to the Work of God'?

Benedict suggests that if we begin to recognize the new life given us in Christ, we will end by opening ourselves to the promise of unending life in our real homeland, the one we cannot yet see. Here he is perhaps most radical and least congenial to the modern bias toward immediate results. Anyone who speaks of heaven is open to the charge of neglecting the realities of life in this world. Is that a fair charge against Benedict? It is true that Benedictines are not always as engaged with the work for justice as they could be. Otherworldliness can be the theological veneer of the terrible vice of monastic complacency. At the same time, monastic life has always pointed to the 'something more' of the human being who has become fully alive. Monastic men and women are persuaded that there is a pearl of great price worth selling everything to obtain. This is a precious witness.

The *Rule* suggests that a monastery's primary focus will be its own communal life, with room made for guests and pilgrims. Anyone who has lived in community knows that little of the human condition is left behind at the gate. Benedict's sensitivity to the dynamics of the common life makes clear his own experience of human frailty. Even so, Benedictines must always guard against forgetting the pains of the world in which they live. Monasteries that have broadened Benedict's perspective to include external works may seem less prone to this danger than more cloistered communities, but as always the issue is attitudinal. Busyness can be the best of blinders for pastoral minister or scribe alike.

Benedict's 'little rule for beginners' adapts its invitation to the circumstances in which each one of us lives. A teacher and model for monastic men and women for centuries, he has become a wise friend to everyone who 'yearns for life and longs to see good days' (*RB* Prol. 15, quoting Ps. 34:12). As always, one must listen in order to learn.

NOTES

CHAPTER 1: UNDERSTANDING BENEDICT

1. For an overview see the historical introduction by Claude Peifer in *RB 1980*, pp. 3–64, and Chitty's *The Desert a City*. These must be complemented by works such as Susanna Elm's *Virgins of God* that highlight the practice of the ascetical life by women.
2. See the various collections of sayings and stories under the heading of *Apophthegmata patrum* in the list of Recommended Reading.
3. Traditionally 'monasticism' has been understood to begin in the fourth century as canonical texts and founders emerge to establish models or movements. To many scholars today, however, the word 'monasticism' has institutional and, more specifically, ecclesiastical, overtones that emphasize the major male figures and their traditions to the exclusion of other models. They generally prefer the more inclusive term 'asceticism' for the early period. By the time of Benedict, however, both the terminology used by ascetics themselves and the ecclesiastical integration of asceticism had advanced to the point that the term 'monasticism' is usually applied to both male and female forms of ascetical life.
4. On Cassian, see my study, *Cassian the Monk*.
5. For an overview of the relationship between *RM* and *RB*, see *RB 1980*, 69–73, 79–90.
6. See *RB 1980's* 'Indexes of Patristic and Ancient Works in *RB*'.
7. The combination of prayer and tears recurs throughout his *Rule*: *RB* 4.57, 20.3, 49.4, 52.4.
8. See the *First Sahidic Life* of Pachomius in Veilleux, *Pachomian Koinonia I*, pp. 430–8.
9. Gregory – like his brother, Basil the Great – regarded his sister Macrina to be his teacher in the spiritual life. He wrote her *Life* and presents his treatise *On the Soul and the Resurrection* in the form of a dialogue with her.
10. Emphasized by Kardong in *Benedict's Rule*, 139–40.
11. *RB* 4.49, 5.18, 7.13–18, 23, 26–9, 19.1.
12. *RB* 4.50, 4.57, 7.44–8, 46.1–6.
13. *RB* 4.21, 5.2, 72.11.

14. *RB* 4.21, 4.72, 7.69, 63.13; cf. 7.34.

CHAPTER 2: WAYS OF PRAYER AND MINDFULNESS

1. Smaragdus, *Expositio* 3.48.13, quoting *Regula Waldeberti* 12 (*CCM* 8:273).
2. Cassian, *Institutes* 2.7–10; cf. *RM* 48.10–11.
3. See Vogüé, *The Rule of Saint Benedict: A Doctrinal and Spiritual Commentary*, 142–9, and Joseph Dyer, 'Monastic Psalmody of the Middle Ages', *Revue Bénédictine* 99 (1989), 41–74.
4. *Expositio*, ch. 48, p. 316.
5. On Cluny, see Lawrence, *Medieval Monasticism*, 86–110 (with bibliography), and Noreen Hunt, *Cluny under Saint Hugh, 1049–1109* (London: Arnold, 1967; Notre Dame, Ind.: Univ. of Notre Dame, 1968).
6. See Hollermann, *The Reshaping of a Tradition*, 292–6.
7. Thus Benedict's concern that those who read in the dormitory during the siesta do so quietly (*RB* 48.5).
8. This phrase occurs in the eighth-century *Memoriale qualiter* (*CCM* 1:251) and was included in the thirteenth-century *Statuta Casinensia* 48 (*CCM* 6:216). Common *lectio* is in the eighth-century *Ordo Casinensis I* 3 (CCM 1:101) and described in many of the medieval customaries. Smaragdus depicts the nightly common reading as a time when questions can be answered and obscure texts explained (*Expositio* 3.42 [*CCM* 8:263, ll. 8–11]).
9. The verb *vacare* occurs throughout *RB* 48.
10. The *Rule of the Four Fathers* 3.10, translated with the other Lerinian Rules in Franklin *et al.*, *Early Monastic Rules*.
11. *Eynsham Customary* 43 (*CCM* 2:53).
12. *Eynsham Customary* 39 (*CCM* 2:51).
13. *Theodomari epistula ad Theodoricum* 20, as in *CCM* 1:134.
14. See the 'Indexes of Patristic and Ancient Works in *RB*' in *RB* 1980, 594–607. Most significant are the references for the chapters Benedict did not adapt from *RM*, for they give us a sense of Benedict's own reading.
15. *Commentationes sive Statuta Murbacensia*, as in *CCM* 1:442. On monastic *florilegia*, see Leclercq, *The Love of Learning and Desire for God*, 228–32. Later lists of texts to be read aloud in community gave pride of place to Gregory the Great's *Dialogues* and *Moral Instructions on Job*, Isidore's *Sentences* on the vices and virtues, Cassian's works, John Chrysostom's sermons, Smaragdus' *Crown of the Monks*. See Donatella Nebbiai-Dalla Guarda, 'Les listes médiévales de lectures monastiques', *Revue Bénédictine* 96 (1986), 271–326. For an evocation of the general atmosphere of medieval monastic reading, see Leclercq's *Love of Learning and Desire for God*, chs. 5–6, 'Sacred Learning' and 'The Ancient Traditional Spirituality' (pp. 87–138). On medieval libraries in English monasteries of women, see David Bell's

What Nuns Read, Cistercian Studies Series 158 (Kalamazoo, Mich.: Cistercian, 1995).

16. *CCM* 1:449, ll. 19–20.

17. See the article on '*Lectio divina* et lecture spirituelle' in the *Dictionnaire de Spiritualité*, 9:470–510, and F. Vandenbroucke, 'La lectio divina du XIe au XIVe siècle', *Studia Monastica* 8 (1966), 267–93.

18. For a balanced introduction, see Casey's *Sacred Reading: The Ancient Art of Lectio Divina*.

19. Quoted by Evagrius, *Praktikos* 92.

20. See George Lindbeck's 'Scripture, Consensus and Community', *This World* 23 (1988), 5–24, and Andrew Louth's chapter on 'Return to Allegory' in *Discerning the Mystery: An Essay on the Nature of Theology* (Oxford: Clarendon, 1983), 96–131.

21. One sees allowance for teaching during the morning *lectio* period in *Ordo Casinensis I* 3, as in *CCM* 1:101.

22. Already a concern in the eighth-century Murbach commentary on the first Synod of Aachen, as in *CCM* 1:449, ll. 24–5. On literacy and Latin in communities of women, see Parisse, *Les nonnes au Moyen Âge*, 165–9, and the observations of Johnson (partly in response to Parisse) in *Equal in Monastic Profession*, 144–7; Bell, *What Nuns Read*, 57–96.

23. Jerome's dream is recounted in his *Letter 22*. See also Cassian's *Conference* 14.12–19 on the dangers of the wrong kind of reading and of presuming to teach.

24. Pope Benedict XII issued decrees for both Benedictine and Cistercians; see the discussion by Vandenbroucke in 'La lectio divina du XIe au XIVe siècle' (as in n.17 above), 267–93, esp. 271–4.

25. See Abelard's reply to Heloise (Letter 7), as in Radice, *The Letters of Abelard and Heloise*, 260–9.

26. The most readable accounts of the Maurists are those of Butler in *Benedictine Monachism*, 337–52, and David Knowles in *Great Historical Enterprises* (London: Thomas Nelson and Sons, 1963), 34–62 (for the number of scholars among the Maurists, see p. 41).

27. Letter of 6 Feb. 1678 to Antoine de Somont, Abbot of Tamié, tr. A.J. Krailsheimer in *The Letters of Armand-Jean de Rancé* (Kalamazoo: Cistercian, 1984), 169.

28. Rancé's interpretation of monastic life, *De la sainteté et des devoirs de la vie monastique* (1683), and Mabillon's treatise have been reprinted (Farnborough, Hants.: Gregg, 1972 and 1967, respectively) but neither has been translated into English. For Rancé, see the biography by A.J. Krailsheimer, *Armand-Jean de Rancé: Abbot of La Trappe* (Oxford: Clarendon, 1974); his letters have been edited and many of them translated by Krailsheimer. On Mabillon, see Knowles' article cited in the previous note as well as his 'Mabillon', *Journal of Ecclesiastical History* 10 (1959), 153–73, reprinted in *The Historian and Character and Other Essays* (Cambridge: CUP, 1963), 213–39.

29. The Liturgical Movement has been associated particularly with the Abbey of Maria Laach in Germany and my own monastery of Saint John's Abbey in the United States. The French, German, and Belgian Benedictines have been active in the emphasis on early Christian studies.

30. Thus the writings of figures as diverse as Thomas Merton, André Louf, and Michael Casey among the Cistercians; Bede Griffiths, John Main, Maria Boulding, and Joan Chittister among the Benedictines.

31. *RB* 38.10 and 63.4, interpreted in light of *RM* 21.1–7 and 24.14; see Nathan Mitchell, 'The Liturgical Code in the Rule of Benedict', in *RB 1980*, 410–12.

32. Women had an analogous division of communities into choir nuns and lay sisters, though the distinction was of social class rather than clerical status.

33. *Ordo Casinensis I* 5, as in *CCM* 1:102; *Theodomari Epistula ad Theodoricum* 21, as in *CCM* 1:134.

34. *RB* 4.72, 27.4, 28.4, 35.15, 38.2, 44.4, 53.4, 58.23, 67.1–2 and 4.

35. *Eynsham Customary* 39 (*CCM* 2:51).

36. On Cassian's teaching and its background, see chapter 6 of my *Cassian the Monk*.

37. The roots of this tradition are in the monologistic prayer described above. The text of the Jesus Prayer, 'Lord Jesus Christ, Son of God, have mercy on me, a sinner' (the last phrase is not always used) first appeared in the sixth or seventh century, though Diadochus of Photike had written in the fifth century about invocation of the name of Jesus.

38. *RB* 4.56–7, 20.3–4, 49.4, 52.4.

39. See Irénée Hausherr's *Penthos: the Doctrine of Compunction in the Christian East* (Kalamazoo: Cistercian, 1982) and Maggie Ross' *The Fountain and the Furnace: the Way of Tears and Fire* (New York: Paulist, 1987).

40. Abba Arsenius, as in the Alphabetical Collection of the *Apophthegmata patrum*, tr. Ward, p. 16.

41. *RB* 38.5, 42.8–11, 52.3–5.

42. Though it is supplemented by *RB* 7.56–61, which recapitulates the main themes of *RB* 6.

43. Cf. *RB* 4.40, 4.51–4, 7.59, 43.8, 48.18, 49.7, 67.5.

44. See *RB* 7.60, 31.7, 61.4, 65.14.

CHAPTER 3: OBEDIENCE AND HUMILITY

1. Cf. *RB* 2.4–5, 3.7 and 11, 64.20.

2. See Kardong, *Benedict's Rule*, 598–602, for an overview of the various approaches.

3. *Expositio Regulae*, 623.

4. Hyperechios 4 in the Alphabetical Collection of the *Apophthegmata patrum*, tr. Ward, p. 200.

5. The Master wrote about those who complain about having to travel (*RM* 57.14); Benedict seemed (more realistically) concerned about the opposite possibility (*RB* 67). The Master also noted that monks will murmur about guests who loll about without working (*RM* 78.12). Benedict's conception of monastic hospitality is completely different from the Master's suspicion of guests.

6. *Institutes* 8.19 and *Conference* 19.12–14.

7. No. 69 of the Anonymous Collection of *Apophthegmata patrum*, tr. Ward in *The Wisdom of the Desert Fathers*, 23.

8. *RB* 60.6–7, though cf. 21.4, 38.12, 64.2.

9. *RB* 2.19, 63.1; cf. 61.11–12, 62.6.

10. *RB* 2.18, 63.8; cf. 54.1–2, 59.6.

CHAPTER 4: THE SHAPE OF CENOBITIC LIFE

1. See, e.g., *The Life of Antony* 7, 16, 19, 91.

2. Concern for cloister runs throughout the text, which can be consulted in McCarthy's translation.

3. For a review of the historical background, see Noreen Hunt, 'Enclosure (II)', *Cistercian Studies* 22 (1987), 126–51; for comments on practice in France, see Johnson, *Equal in Monastic Profession*, 150–63.

4. For the American experience, see Hollermann, *The Reshaping of a Tradition*, 234–7, 239–41.

5. *RB* 4.40: 'do not speak ill of others'; 69–72: 'Shun arrogance. Respect the seniors, love the juniors. Pray for your enemies out of love for Christ.'

6. *Praktikos* 12.

7. Saying Poemen 174 from the Alphabetical Collection of *Apophthegmata patrum*, tr. Ward, *The Sayings of the Desert Fathers*, 160–1.

8. See the First Sahidic Life of Pachomius, as in Veilleux's *Pachomian Koinonia I*, 430–7.

9. Preserved in a late form in Veilleux's *Pachomian Koinonia II*, 141–95.

10. For an overview of this process, see Adalbert de Vogüé, '*Sub regula vel abbate*', in *Rule and Life: An Interdisciplinary Symposium*, ed. M. Basil Pennington, Cistercian Studies Series 12 (Spencer, Ma.: Cistercian, 1971), 21–63.

11. See Lawless' edition and translation of Augustine's *Praeceptum*.

12. Translated by Franklin *et al.* in *Early Monastic Rules*.

13. For a survey of the various Latin rules, see Vogüé's 'The Cenobitic Rules of the West', *Cistercian Studies* 12 (1977), 177–83, and Mary Forman and Thomas Sullivan, 'The Latin Cenobitic Rules: AD 400–700: Editions and Translations', *American Benedictine Review*

48 (1997), 52–68. On the diffusion of *RB*, see the summary in *RB 1980*, 113–131.

14. For a readable and brief survey of this process and later developments, see Lawrence's *Medieval Monasticism*. Lawrence's study should be supplemented by Johnson's *Equal in Monastic Profession* or Parisse's *Les nonnes au Moyen Âge* for female monasticism.

15. Prefaced by an exhortation to unity (the *Obiurgatio*). Both the *Obiurgatio* and the feminine version of the *Praeceptum* are translated by Lawless in *Augustine of Hippo and His Monastic Rule*, 104–18.

16. Donatus' *Rule for Virgins* (7th century) is an example of a *regula mixta* for women; it combines the rules of Caesarius, Benedict, and Columban. See the translation in McNamara and Halborg, *The Ordeal of Community*.

17. The oldest extant copy is from the eleventh century. See J. Frank Henderson, 'Feminizing the Rule of Benedict in Medieval England', *Magistra* 1 (1995), 9–38. For English examples from the fifteenth century, see Ernst A. Kock, *Three Middle English Versions of the Rule of St. Benet* (London: Early English Text Society, 1902).

18. Their correspondence is translated by Radice in *The Letters of Abelard and Heloise*, 159–269 (Letters 5–7).

19. Those independent monasteries which for historical or canonical reasons do not have an abbot or abbess have a prior or prioress who fulfils the same role as Benedict's abbot. Almost all monasteries of Benedictine women in North America, for example, are led by prioresses who have the same responsibilities and authority as their European sisters who are abbesses. Such priors/prioresses should not be confused with Benedict's 'prior' (*praepositus*), who occupies the second place in the community and helps the abbot.

20. *RB* 3.11, 64.20.

21. *RB* 2.1–4, 30; 27 *passim*.

22. *RB* 2.1, 6–10, 30–40; 3.11; 27.5–9; 64.7.

23. *RB* 2.17, 22; 27.18–19; 64.11.

24. Hildemar, *Expositio*, ch. 2, pp. 87–8.

25. See esp. *RB* 2.33–4, 39–40; 64.2.

26. *RB* 2.11–15 and 23–9.

27. *RB* 64.17–19; cf. 2.31–2; 27 *passim*; 28.2; 64.12–14.

28. For this theme, see *RB* 34.5, 41.5, 65.11.

29. *RB* 35.13 (snack for kitchen servers), 39.6 (extra food for heavy work), 40.5 (extra wine for heavy work or thirst), 41.4–5 (times for meals), 53.18 (extra help in the kitchen for guests), 55.8 (ensuring that clothes fit properly), 63 *passim* (rank).

30. *RB* 36.4–6, 10 (the sick); 27 (the excommunicated); 53, 56 (guests).

31. *RB* 47.1 (signal for divine office); 49.8, 10 (Lenten resolutions); 49.24–5, 57 (assigns tasks).

32. *RB* 22.2 (bedding); 32–3 (material goods of the monastery); 54 (gifts); 55 (clothing and footwear).

33. *RB* 21 (deans), 31 (cellarer), 65 (prior).
34. See Johnson, *Equal in Monastic Profession*, 166–73; Parisse, *Les nonnes au Moyen Âge*, 116–22; the overview in Jean Gaudemet, *Les élections dans l'église latine des origines au XVIe siècle* (Paris: Lanore, 1979), 215–305.
35. *Letter* 7, tr. Radice, p. 202.
36. American Benedictine women have elected term superiors since their arrival in the mid-nineteenth century; the original reason for this practice is now unclear. See Hollermann, *The Reshaping of a Tradition*, 254–8.

CHAPTER 5: THE DISCIPLINED LIFE

1. See *RB* 8–11 and Kardong's commentary in *Benedict's Rule*, 212–13.
2. For Benedict's dietary regulations, see *RB* 39–40. According to *RB* 36.9, the very ill were allowed meat. To Benedict's approach we can compare that of the Master, who legislated that those who claimed to be sick should be given minimal nourishment as a way to discourage shirkers (*RM* 69.2–3)! At Monte Cassino in the eighth century, an extra cooked dish had been added and there was provision for a snack in the late afternoon during the summer; fowl was eaten only for major feasts (*Theodomari epistula ad Karolum regem*, as in *CCM* 1:165–6). The first Synod of Aachen forbade the eating of fowl except by the sick; the second allowed it for Christmas and Easter. See *CCM* 1:458 (with helpful note) and 481.
3. See Kardong's analysis in *Benedict's Rule*, 308–9. The first Synod of Aachen allowed baths at Christmas and Easter (as in *CCM* 1:459). Of course, bathing is not the only way to keep clean, and Benedict expects his monks to wash both feet and hands (*RB* 35.8).
4. Although vows of poverty and chastity have sometimes been added to the traditional Benedictine vow formula for the sake of similarity to the promises of other religious orders.
5. *RB* 33.4, cf. 58.25. The theme of renouncing self-will runs throughout the Prologue, *RB* 5 ('Obedience') and 7 ('Humility').
6. *Institutes* 7.7, 9–10, paraphrase.
7. *RB* 22.2 (bedding); 31.4–5, 15 (cellarer reports to and obeys the superior); 32.3 (inventory of goods); 33 (all goods from the superior); 54 (letters and gifts); 55 (clothing, footwear, bedding and other necessary items).
8. *Praeceptum*, 1.5–7.
9. Arsenius 36 of the Alphabetical Collection of the *Apophthegmata patrum*, tr. Ward, p. 14.
10. *RB* 39.6, 40.5, 48.7–8; cf. *RM* 86, which requires that fields be leased to others and monks prevented from heavy labour lest it distract them from their prayer and interfere with their fasting.
11. See Kardong's remarks in *Benedict's Rule*, 398–9.

12. *RB* 4.64, 'love chastity'; 64.9, the superior must be chaste, temperate and merciful; 72.8, the members of the community must show chaste love to one another. There may well be some practical concerns about chastity in the rules about sleeping arrangements (*RB* 21.1, 7) and bathing (*RB* 36.8).

13. *RB* 64.11 and 15, 72.10.

14. *The Mirror of Charity* and *Spiritual Friendship*, as in the list of Recommended Reading.

15. *Ordo Casinensis I, CCM* 1:104.

16. On seeking a spiritual elder for help in discernment, see Columba Stewart, 'Radical Honesty about the Self', *Sobornost* 12 (1990), 25–39 and 143–56; these articles were reprinted as 'The Desert Fathers on Radical Self-Honesty' in *Vox Benedictina* 8 (1991), 7–53; also in *A.I.M. Monastic Bulletin*, English edition, nos. 63–4 (1997–8). On the sayings of the elders, see the entries under *Apophthegmata patrum* in the Bibliography.

17. See Columba Stewart, 'Manifestation of Thoughts in the Rule of Benedict', *Studia Patristica* 25 (1993) 451–6.

18. In *RB* 4.50 the phrase about disclosure was added to the source, *RM* 3.56; *RB* 46.5 has no parallel in *RM*. The Master devotes an entire chapter (*RM* 15) to manifestation of thoughts and the system by which thoughts were brought to the abbot's attention by the deans.

19. See Stewart, 'Manifestation of Thoughts in the *Rule of Benedict*', 453–4.

20. *Expositio in Regulam S. Benedicti* 7, pp. 153–4.

21. See Cassian's *Institutes* 5–12 and *Conference* 5. The system comes from Evagrius Ponticus, who outlines it in the first part of the *Praktikos*.

22. See Donatus' prescription in ch. 23 of the *Rule for Virgins* (tr. McNamara and Halborg, p. 51).

23. *Memoriale qualiter*, 'Exhortationes de bona observantia' (*CCM* 1:249).

24. Commenting on *RB* 4.50, *Expositio*, p. 171.

25. See *Memoriale qualiter* 5 (*CCM* 1:234); cf. *Theodomari epistula ad Theodoricum* 23 (*CCM* 1:134).

26. *RB* 46.1–3; *Memoriale qualiter* 7 (*CCM* 1:237–8) and also in the later adaptation for women (*CCM* 1:269–71).

27. *Regularis Concordia Anglicae Nationis* 27 (*CCM* 7/3, p. 88; cf. the similar point in *Aelfrici Epistula* 7, p. 157).

28. *Eynsham Customary* 117–18 (*CCM* 2:79).

CHAPTER 6: TIMES AND SEASONS OF BENEDICTINE LIFE

1. For the *Opus Dei*, November 1 (All Saints) was the calendrical counterpoint to Easter (*RB* 8); for meals, Easter, Pentecost, September 13 (vigil of Triumph of the Cross) and the start of Lent marked the

various seasons (*RB* 41–2); for work and *lectio*, Easter, October 1 and the start of Lent were days when the schedule changed (*RB* 48).

2. Although he reminds the superior to 'seek first the kingdom of God and his righteousness [Matt. 6:33]' (*RB* 2.35).

3. *RB* 58.4, 9–10 suggests (especially when read in light of *RM* 88.7–10) that the newcomer spend two months in the guest quarters before entering the novitiate. Hildemar read it this way, seeing the two months under the guestmaster's tutelage as a sort of postulancy (*Expositio*, pp. 434–5).

4. See *Statuta Petri Venerabilis* 37 (*CCM* 6:71).

5. A nineteenth-century development in monastic congregations. For example, choir monks in the American–Cassinese Congregation of male Benedictines made solemn vows after the novitiate until 1892. In that year, 'simple perpetual' vows were introduced, to be followed after three years by solemn vows. The difference was one of canonical status and disposition of property, not of duration: both were permanent, lifetime commitments. In the early twentieth century this was changed again to three years of temporary vows followed by solemn vows for choir monks and perpetual simple vows for lay brothers. As explained later in this chapter, the distinction between the two kinds of monks was abolished in the 1960s.

6. For the evolution of the rites to the twelfth century, see Giles Constable, 'The Ceremonies and Symbolism of Entering Religious Life, from the Fourth to the Twelfth Century', in *Segni e riti nella chiesa altomedievale occidentale*, Settimane di studio del Centro Italiano di Studi sull' alto medioevo, 33:2 (Spoleto: Presso la Sede del Centro, 1987), pp. 771–834.

7. See *RB* 1.7 and Constable, 'The Ceremonies and Symbolism', 796. Samaragdus includes a prayer before tonsure, *Expositio* 58.26 (*CCM* 8:298).

8. Constable, 'The Ceremonies and Symbolism', 810–12, and modern Benedictine practice. Hildemar has the (male) novice clothed in 'clerical garb', i.e. the tunic or cassock, after two months and then given the cowl at profession (*Expositio*, pp. 536 and 547).

9. On this ancient custom which was common through the fifteenth century and revived in the nineteenth, see Rene Metz, *La consécration des vierges dans l'Église romaine* (Paris: Presses universitaires de France, 1954). The rite was reformed after Vatican II and is now much less frequently used. The relationship between monastic profession and consecration of virgins is unclear for the early Benedictine centuries; the decline of the practice by the sixteenth century is attributed by Metz to the significance of the profession ceremony itself which included key elements of the consecration ceremony such as veiling and conferral of a ring. When Guéranger revived the consecration for the nuns at Sainte-Cécile in 1868, profession and

consecration were done at the same ceremony. Other congregations celebrated the consecration several years after profession.

10. See the discussion in Chapter 4 on enclosure.

11. The eschatological dimension is most prominent at the beginning and end of *RB* (Prol. ch. 7 and chs. 72–3).

12. See *RM* 10.93–117; the details include the predictable ones of good weather, fine music, fragrant flowers as well as the note that 'there the food causes no excrement' (*RM* 10.11), something to look forward to in an age without plumbing.

13. Most notably in *RB* Prol. 49 and in the way that Benedict de-emphasizes the eschatological framework of *RM* 10 (= *RB* 7).

RECOMMENDED READING

Monastic Texts Cited in this Study:

Abelard, *Letters to Heloise* (12th century), tr. Betty Radice, *The Letters of Abelard and Heloise* (Harmondsworth, Middlesex: Penguin, 1974).

Aelred of Rievaulx (12th century), *The Mirror of Charity*, tr. Elizabeth Connor, Cistercian Fathers 17 (Kalamazoo, Mich.: Cistercian, 1990).
  Spiritual Friendship, tr. Mary Eugenia Laker, Cistercian Fathers 5 (Kalamazoo, Mich.: Cistercian, 1974).

Apophthegmata patrum (4th-5th century), Alphabetical Collection, tr. Benedicta Ward, *The Sayings of the Desert Fathers* (Oxford: Mowbray/ Kalamazoo, Mich.: Cistercian, 1975).
  Anonymous Collection, Part 1: tr. Benedicta Ward, *The Wisdom of the Desert Fathers* (Fairacres, Oxford: SLG Press, 1975; new ed. 1986); Part 2: tr. Columba Stewart, *The World of the Desert Fathers* (Fairacres, Oxford: SLG Press, 1986; new ed. 1995).

Athanasius, *The Life of Antony* (4th century), tr. Robert C. Gregg, Classics of Western Spirituality (New York: Paulist, 1980).

Augustine, *Praeceptum* (4th century), ed. and tr. George Lawless, *Augustine of Hippo and His Monastic Rule* (Oxford: Clarendon, 1987), pp. 80-103.

Basil the Great, *Long Rules* (4th century), tr. (1) W.K.L. Clarke, *The Ascetic Works of Saint Basil* (London: SPCK, 1925), pp. 145-228; (2) M. Monica Wagner, *Saint Basil: Ascetical Works*, Fathers of the Church (New York: Fathers of the Church, 1950), pp. 223-337.
  Short Rules, tr. Clarke, *The Ascetic Works of Saint Basil*, pp. 229-351.

Caesarius of Arles, *Rule for Virgins* (6th century), tr. Maria Caritas McCarthy, *The Rule for Nuns of St. Caesarius of Arles: a Translation with a Critical Introduction*, Catholic University of America, Studies in Mediaeval History, new series, v. 16 (Washington: Catholic University Press, 1960).

Donatus of Besançon, *Rule for Virgins* (7th century), tr. Jo Ann McNamara and John Halborg in *The Ordeal of Community* (Toronto: Peregrina, n.d.).

Evagrius Ponticus, *Praktikos* (4th century), tr. John Eudes Bamberger,

Evagrius Ponticus: Praktikos and Chapters on Prayer, Cistercian Studies Series 4 (Kalamazoo, Mich.: Cistercian, 1972), pp. 12-42.

Gregory the Great, *Dialogues* (7th century), tr. Odo John Zimmerman, Fathers of the Church 39 (New York: Fathers of the Church, 1959).

Gregory of Nyssa, *Life of Macrina* (4th century), tr. Kevin Corrigan (Toronto: Peregrina, 1987).

Heloise, *Letters to Abelard* (12th century), tr. Betty Radice, *The Letters of Abelard and Heloise* (Harmondsworth, Middlesex: Penguin, 1974).

Jerome, *Letters* (4th century), tr. Charles Christopher Mierow, Ancient Christian Writers 33 (Westminster, Maryland: Newman Press, 1963).

John Cassian, *Conferences* (5th century), tr. (1) E.C.S. Gibson, Library of Nicene and Post-Nicene Fathers, Second Series, vol. 11, pp. 293-545 (omits *Conf.* 12 and 22); (2) Boniface Ramsey, *John Cassian: the Conferences*, Ancient Christian Writers 57 (Mahwah, N.J.: Paulist, 1997).

Institutes, tr. E.C.S. Gibson, Library of Nicene and Post-Nicene Fathers, Second Series, vol. 11, pp. 199-290 (omits *Inst.* 6).

Lerinian Rules (5th century), Latin text and English tr. Carmela Vircillo Franklin, Ivan Havener, J. Alcuin Francis, *Early Monastic Rules* (Collegeville, Minn.: Liturgical Press, 1982).

Pachomius, *Lives, Rules*, and other documents (4th century), tr. Armand Veilleux, *Pachomian Koinonia I–III*, Cistercian Studies Series 45-47 (Kalamazoo, Mich.: Cistercian, 1980-2).

Rule of the Master (6th century), tr. Luke Eberle, Cistercian Studies Series 6 (Kalamazoo, Mich.: Cistercian, 1977).

Editions of the Rule of Benedict and Early Commentaries Cited in this Study:

Benedict of Nursia, *Rule* (6th century), ed. Timothy Fry *et al.*, *RB 1980: The Rule of St. Benedict in Latin and English with Notes* (Collegeville, Minn.: Liturgical Press, 1981).

Bernard of Monte Cassino, *Expositio in Regulam S. Benedicti* (12th century), ed. Anselm Caplet (Monte Cassino: Typographia Montis Casini, 1894).

Hildemar, *Expositio Regulae ab Hildemaro Tradita et Nunc Primum Typis Mandata* (9th century), in *Vita et Regula SS.P. Benedicti Una Cum Expositione Regulae*, vol. 3 (Ratisbon: Pustet, 1880).

Smaragdus, *Expositio in Regulam S. Benedicti* (9th century), ed. Alfred Spannagel and Pius Engelbert, *CCM* 8 (Siegburg [Germany]: Franz Schmitt, 1974).

Modern Studies of Monastic Life and Spirituality:

Butler, Cuthbert, *Benedictine Monachism*, 2nd ed. with supplementary notes (London/New York: Longmans, 1924).

Casey, Michael, *Sacred Reading: The Ancient Art of Lectio Divina* (Liguori, Missouri: Triumph Books, 1995).

Toward God: The Ancient Wisdom of Western Prayer (Liguori, Missouri: Triumph Books, 1996).

Chittister, Joan D., *The Rule of Benedict: Insights for the Ages* (New York: Crossroad, 1992).

Chitty, Derwas, *The Desert a City: An Introduction to the Study of Egyptian and Palestinian Monasticism under the Christian Empire* (Oxford: Blackwell, 1966; Rpt. Crestwood, New York: St Vladimir's Seminary).

De Waal, Esther, *A Life-Giving Way: A Commentary on the Rule of St. Benedict* (Collegeville, Minn: Liturgical Press, 1995).

Living with Contradiction: Reflections on the Rule of St. Benedict (San Francisco: Harper & Row, 1989).

Seeking God: The Way of St. Benedict (Collegeville, Minn.: Liturgical Press, 1984).

Elm, Susanna, *Virgins of God: The Making of Asceticism in Late Antiquity* (Oxford: Clarendon, 1994).

Hollermann, Ephrem, *The Reshaping of the Tradition: American Benedictine Women, 1852-1881* (Saint Joseph, Minn.: Sisters of the Order of Saint Benedict, 1994).

Johnson, Penelope D., *Equal in Monastic Profession. Religious Women in Medieval France* (Chicago: Univ. of Chicago, 1991).

Kardong, Terrence, *The Benedictines* (Wilmington, Del. [Collegeville, Minn.]: Michael Glazier [Liturgical Press], 1988).

Benedict's Rule: A Translation and Commentary (Collegeville, Minn.: Liturgical Press, 1996).

Lawrence, C. H., *Medieval Monasticism: Forms of Religious Life in Western Europe in the Middle Ages*, 2nd ed. (London/New York: Longmans, 1989).

Leclercq, Jean, *The Love of Learning and the Desire for God: A Study of Monastic Culture*, tr. Catharine Misrahi, 3rd ed. (New York: Fordham University Press, 1982).

Merton, Thomas, *The Climate of Monastic Prayer*, Cistercian Studies Series 1 (Spencer, Mass. [Kalamazoo, Mich.]: Cistercian, 1969).

The Monastic Journey, ed. Patrick Hart, Cistercian Studies Series 133 (Kalamazoo, Mich.: Cistercian, 1992).

Norris, Kathleen, *The Cloister Walk* (New York: Riverhead, 1996).

Dakota: a Spiritual Geography (New York: Ticknor & Fields, 1993).

Parisse, Michel, *Les nonnes au Moyen Âge* (Le Puy [France]: Bonneton, 1983).

Rees, Daniel, *et al.*, *Consider Your Call. A Theology of the Monastic Life Today* (London: SPCK, 1978/Kalamazoo, Mich.: Cistercian, 1980).

Stewart, Columba, *Cassian the Monk* (New York: Oxford, 1998).

Vogüé, Adalbert de, *The Rule of Saint Benedict: A Doctrinal and Spiritual Commentary,* tr. John Baptist Hasbrouck, Cistercian Studies Series 54 (Kalamazoo, Mich.: Cistercian, 1983).